Key Thinkers in Christianity

Key Thinkers in Christianity

edited by

ADRIAN HASTINGS
ALISTAIR MASON
& HUGH PYPER

OXFORD
UNIVERSITY PRESS

OXFORD
UNIVERSITY PRESS

Great Clarendon Street, Oxford OX2 6DP

Oxford University Press is a department of the University of Oxford.
It furthers the University's objective of excellence in research, scholarship,
and education by publishing worldwide in

Oxford   New York

Auckland   Bangkok   Buenos Aires   Cape Town   Chennai
Dar es Salaam   Delhi   Hong Kong   Istanbul   Karachi   Kolkata
Kuala Lumpur   Madrid   Melbourne   Mexico City   Mumbai   Nairobi
São Paulo   Shanghai   Taipei   Tokyo   Toronto

Oxford is a registered trade mark of Oxford University Press
in the UK and in certain other countries

Published in the United States
by Oxford University Press Inc., New York

© Oxford University Press 2003

Database right Oxford University Press (maker)

First published 2003

British Library Cataloguing in Publication Data

Data available

Library of Congress Cataloging in Publication Data

Data available

ISBN 0–19–280279–8

2

Typeset in Pondicherry, India, by
Alliance Interactive Technology
Printed in Great Britain by
Clays Ltd
Bungay, Suffolk

Contents

Contents

Introduction

Who are the twenty or so key thinkers in Christianity? Beyond some inescapable names, further selection is inevitably a matter of judgement. The present list was drawn up by Adrian Hastings not long before his death in May 2001. He drew on the articles on major thinkers in *The Oxford Companion to Christian Thought*, which I was privileged to edit with him and Alistair Mason. With his encyclopaedic knowledge of Christian history and wide ecumenical and international sympathies, Adrian was the first to regret the names not included and to be aware of the voices that are not heard here. One obvious omission was deliberate: he opted not to include the writers of the New Testament period, great thinkers though they are, but to begin when a self-conscious tradition of Christian thought starts to reflect on its own identity and development.

It is undeniable that the key thinkers in this selection are all dead, almost all European, and all men. The lack of living figures can be defended: it is only as subsequent generations find a body of thought inescapable because of the answers or, more likely, the questions it encapsulates that its enduring significance begins to come clear. The ideas these thinkers put forward are far from dead, and it is the vitality of the tradition which they represent which justifies their inclusion. The jury may still be out on some 20th-century figures.

The other points are harder to counter. At the dawn of the 21st century, we are increasingly aware of the many women and many people beyond Europe throughout Christian history who, if there were any justice, should be included in the list of its key thinkers. There, of course, is the rub. These things are not, and have not been, just. Including token names only emphasizes the point. Let us hope that the editors of any such volume a century from now will find that the names of Christian thinkers who speak for the majority of humanity, woefully under-represented in this list, spring incontestably and irresistibly to mind. We are not quite there yet.

There is a subtle difference between a list of a tradition's greatest thinkers and its key thinkers, although in many cases the two will coincide. The members of this list were chosen not only for the brilliance and originality of their thought, but because they are the ones to whom other thinkers go back, sometimes as the representatives of an age or a way of thinking rather than simply through their individual contribution.

Men of their time they may be, but each of them still speaks to contemporary readers and their books are still read. Whatever one may think of their conclusions or assumptions, it is impossible to engage with their writings and not come away awed by the sheer intellectual power they manifest. Thought about things spiritual is unfashionable these days, all too often being replaced either by an easy relativism that cannot sustain the tolerance it espouses or by a defensive dogmatism. Of course we need to remember that thought and wisdom are not the same; neither are wisdom and ignorance.

These thinkers remind us that, for much of Christian history, the brilliant minds which nowadays may be attracted to wrestling with ultimate questions in cosmology, quantum physics, or molecular genetics found their intellectual challenge in the complexities and subtleties of theology. Mastery of a complex and ever-developing tradition, an ability to think within that tradition and yet to draw on the developments of the wider culture and to speak to it, and a profound understanding of what it is to be human inform them all. Like all great thinkers, even when they are wrong, they are far more interesting and illuminating than most of the rest of us when we are right.

They are not just theologians in some narrow sense, either. Many of the ideas honed by their attempts to think through the paradoxes of the Christian life have shaped our understanding of philosophy, psychology, and politics, to mention only a few of the areas they influence. Moreover, for each of them, what they thought and wrote about was not simply an academic exercise, but a truth which shaped how they lived and for which many of them were prepared to suffer. A hunger for integrity of thought and life in response to the mystery of the Christian God characterizes them, and an awareness, too, of the dangers and limitations of human cleverness.

It is important to set each of these figures against their social and intellectual background. As Adrian Hastings wrote in the introduction to *The Oxford Companion to Christian Thought*, while Christian thought depends on the contribution of individuals, it is also 'a matter of the complex and subtle histories of works and ideas, institutional doctrines, popular devotion, artistic imagination, all of this caught up in humanity's long march across the centuries in search of the meaning of things'. The partner volume to this one, *Christian Thought: A Brief History*, will supply the context for their work and interested reader should refer further to the *Companion* and to other works such as *The Oxford Dictionary of the Christian Church*.

The present volume dips into a great well of dedicated scholarship and careful editing to which many people have contributed. Adrian Hastings's thanks to the contributors, the editorial team, and to Oxford University Press are warmly echoed here. The clarity, economy, and rigour of the chapters in this book are testimony to his outstanding editorial gifts: incisive efficiency, persistence, passion, and scholarship.

This volume will be a fitting testimonial to Adrian's work if it conveys some of the excitement of applying the marvellous resources of the human mind to the perennial and unfathomable mysteries of human existence and the seemingly inexhaustible resonances of the Christian tradition. If it sends readers back to the writings of these remarkable representatives of that tradition, and inspires some with the courage and humility to engage with the continuing endeavour which is Christian thought, no one would be better pleased than he.

Hugh S. Pyper

Leeds

17 February 2002

Editors and Contributors

Editors

The late ADRIAN HASTINGS was Emeritus Professor of Theology, University of Leeds, and previously Professor of Religious Studies, University of Zimbabwe. He was the Editor of the *Journal of Religion in Africa* for 15 years. He also edited a number of books including *Modern Catholicism* (1991) and *A World History of Christianity* (1999). His many other publications include a two-volume commentary on the documents of the Second Vatican Council (1968–9), *A History of English Christianity 1920–2000* (1986, 3rd edn 2001), *The Theology of a Protestant Catholic* (1990), *Robert Runcie* (1991), *SOS Bosnia* (1993), *The Church in Africa 1450–1950* (1994, a volume in the *Oxford History of the Christian Church*), and *The Construction of Nationhood* (1997).

ALISTAIR MASON has recently retired as Senior Lecturer in Church History, University of Leeds. He is the author of *A History of the Society of the Sacred Mission* (1993), and editor of *Religion in Leeds* (1994).

HUGH PYPER is Head of School and Senior Lecturer in Biblical Studies, University of Leeds. He is the author of *David as Reader: 2 Samuel 12: 1–5 and the Poetics of Fatherhood* (1996), and editor of *The Christian Family: A Concept in Crisis* (1996).

Contributors

EUAN CAMERON, Professor of Early Modern History, University of Newcastle upon Tyne

Abbreviations

The following abbreviations are used in *The Oxford Companion to Christian Thought*. Many of these abbreviations appear in this volume also.

ARCIC	Anglican/Roman Catholic International Commission
c.	circa
CD	Karl Barth, *Church Dogmatics*
col/s.	column/s
d.	died (with date)
DE	Degree on Ecumenism (Vatican II)
DV	Dei Verbum (Vatican II)
EH	Eusebius, *Ecclesiastical History*
ET	English translation
GS	Gaudium et Spes (Vatican II)
LG	Lumen Gentium (Vatican II)
LXX	Septuagint
NT	New Testament
OT	Old Testament
ST	Thomas Aquinas, *Summa Theologiae*
sv.	*sub verbo* (under the word)
vs.	versus

Biblical references

Gen.	Genesis	**1, 2 Sam.**	1, 2 Samuel
Exod.	Exodus	**1, 2 Kgs.**	1, 2 Kings
Lev.	Leviticus	**1, 2 Chr.**	1, 2 Chronicles
Num.	Numbers	**Pss.**	Psalms
Deut.	Deuteronomy	**Prov.**	Proverbs
Josh.	Joshua	**Eccles.**	Ecclesiastes
Judg.	Judges	**Isa.**	Isaiah

Jer.	Jeremiah	**Rom.**	Romans
Ezek.	Ezekiel	**1, 2 Cor.**	1, 2 Corinthians
Dan.	Daniel	**Gal.**	Galatians
Hos.	Hosea	**Eph.**	Ephesians
Mic.	Micah	**Phil.**	Philippians
Zech.	Zechariah	**Col.**	Colossians
Mal.	Malachi	**1, 2 Thess.**	1, 2 Thessalonians
1, 2 Esd.	1, 2 Esdras	**1, 2 Tim.**	1, 2 Timothy
Tob.	Tobit	**Philem.**	Philemon
Wisd.	Wisdom of Solomon	**Heb.**	Hebrews
Ecclus.	Ecclesiasticus	**Jas.**	James
1, 2 Macc.	1, 2 Maccabees	**1, 2 Pet.**	1, 2 Peter
Sir.	Ecclesiaticus	**Rev.**	Revelation
Matt.	Matthew		

Irenaeus (*c.130–c.200*)

HUGH S. PYPER

Irenaeus retains a particular importance in the history of Christian thought as the first exponent of a catholic Christian orthodoxy. In contrast to most earlier Christian writers, his arguments are not directed against Judaism or paganism, but at defining orthodox Christianity against various Gnostic groups, particularly the Valentinians. These groups did acknowledge Jesus as Saviour and claimed to be passing on his secret teachings suppressed by the orthodox church. Irenaeus' *Adversus Haereses* (*Against the Heretics*) remains a vital source of information on the teachings of his opponents although his purpose is not to give a fair or dispassionate summary of their views, which at times he satirizes with some wit.

In the process of revealing the falsity of the Gnostics' claims to represent true Christian teaching, he is the first to give a coherent formulation of Christian doctrine. His concern is not to defend what is distinctive about Christianity against external enemies but to define its core and demonstrate the principles of the internal logic that give it coherence as an all-encompassing system of belief. By doing this he can then show that Gnostic teachings fail these tests of coherence. His own positive synthesis is set out in less polemical terms in his other extant work, *The Demonstration of the Apostolic Teaching*, which was redis-covered as recently as 1904. His expression of what he calls the divine 'economy', by which he means the way in which God's coherent plan of salvation, itself a revelation of the nature of God's being, is worked out, shapes all subsequent Christian thought.

Not much is known of his life. In a letter to the Roman presbyter Florinus, Irenaeus tells us that as a boy he hung on the words of the then aged bishop Polycarp who himself had been a follower of the apostle John. This living link back to the apostolic age is a key to Irenaeus' sense of tradition. The incident implies that Irenaeus was brought up in the vicinity of Smyrna in present-day Turkey. Later, Irenaeus moved to Gaul for some unspecified reason, perhaps connected to missionary work, and became a presbyter in the church at Lugdunum (Lyons). The church there sent him as a representative to Rome. Possibly on his return to Lyons he was appointed bishop. His Asian heritage and Greek edu-cation enabled him to bring to birth what became a distinctively West-ern tradition of thought although he is writing long before the Eastern and Western churches grew apart. Much later traditions report that he met a martyr's death.

Irenaeus' fundamental conviction is that there is a consistent, true tradition of Christian teaching which can be traced back to Jesus through the teaching of the apostles and their appointed successors and that the church's office is to guard and preserve this heritage. Those who seek truth and savation must then turn to the apostolic church which encapsulates the apostolic faith in its baptismal creed. All the various Gnostic claims concerning secret traditions handed down by the apostles but not taught by the apostolic church are wicked fancies. If the apostles had really taught any such oral traditions, whom would they have entrusted them to but the bishops they had appointed as their successors? The ancient churches and their bishops can trace their suc-cession back to the apostles, whereas the Gnostic groups, in Irenaeus' view, demonstrate no such lineage. Pre-eminent among the churches is the Church of Rome, founded by not one but two apostles, Peter and Paul, and maintaining an unbroken succession of bishops. Irenaeus' understanding of the church here clearly sows the seeds for the subsequent development of the papacy, although his point is to defend the existence of an apostolic tradition common to all the churches.

If his understanding of the church is important, so is his role in the development of the Christian bible and its authority. Irenaeus is the first writer who treats the NT books as scriptures on a par with the Hebrew scriptures and he preserves important early traditions about the composition of the gospels and development of the canon. His canon is not quite the modern one, however, as he accepts the Shepherd of Hermas and not the Epistle to the Hebrews. Importantly, he does insist that there must be four and only four gospels, bolstering his argument with analogies from the four winds and the four beasts of the book of Revelation. These gospels must not only have apostolic authorship, but have been accepted by the church. The rapidly growing number of Gnostic gospels in that period are thus ruled out of court.

All this effort to undermine the authority of the Gnostic preachers was the result of his determination to refute their central tenet. Intrinsic to the Gnostic vision as Irenaeus portrays it was a profound dualism between spirit and matter. Human beings were spirit trapped in matter and salvation was to be sought in liberation from matter and from its creator, who was often identified with the God of the OT who was distinguished from the Father of the Word. Gnostic interpretation of the Scriptures involved differentiating between those passages which spoke of spiritual entities and those which were concerned with the world of matter. In particular, passages like the prologue to John's gospel, in which the Word becomes flesh, were interpreted by making a clear distinction between the Word, which was spiritual, and Jesus, who was material. The range of names for God in the OT was a fertile source for the construction of elaborate celestial hierarchies with some scriptural backing.

Irenaeus refutes these approaches. The Creator and the Father are one, and only on this basis is salvation possible. All the titles of the OT refer to this one God. He insists on the importance of the doctrine that creation occurs *ex nihilo*, in opposition to the idea that creation occurs through the action of the demiurge on pre-existent formless matter. Although he does not formulate the classical doctrine of the Trinity, he uses a fundamentally trinitarian scheme to counter the Gnostics. One God, Creator and Father, is revealed in both the Old and New Testaments. The Son and the Spirit, whom he sometimes calls the 'two hands of the Father' are not secondary or created entities, but divine. The Word is Christ who is Jesus. No distinction between them is allowable, as the equivalence of these terms is the point of the mystery of the incarnation. Irenaeus is also firm that there are mysteries of God's being which it is not our business to know, and which we could not comprehend. The heavenly hierarchies of the Gnostics are not just wrong, but claim specious knowledge about things human beings cannot and should not enquire into.

Unlike the Gnostics, who to varying degrees rejected the OT as the record of the inferior doings of the creative Demiurge, he reads the OT as a prophetic record of the coming of the son of God. The Mosaic law is educational, containing concessions to the weakness of the Israelites but also foreshadowing the revelation to come. Irenaeus gives authority to a long-lasting tradition of distinctively Christian exegesis. In contrast to the earlier Christian apologists, he has some sense of the narrative sweep of scripture rather than simply regarding it as a repository of proof-texts, but is also given to some rather strained allegorical interpretations. Where there are difficulties or seeming contradictions in the scriptures, in Irenaeus' view, these are to be reconciled by appealing to the teaching of the apostles and their successors. A plurality of gospels is preserved which can be used to illuminate difficult passages in each other, but these cannot be supplemented by other books. In that sense, the incarnational faith which he espouses is the key to hermeneutics. The untrained reader outside the church is liable to be led astray by uninstructed biblical reading, as obviously has happened to his Gnostic opponents.

The teaching most often associated with Irenaeus is his doctrine of 'recapitulation', a term derived from Eph. 1: 10. In this, he develops the Pauline teaching of Jesus as the second Adam. Adam when first created was, in Irenaeus' view, a spiritual infant whom God sought to train up as a son of God, but who was led into disobedience by the devil. To undo the consequences of this, the Son took flesh from the Virgin Mary to live a life of obedience, reversing at each stage of human life the effects of Adam's transgression. In defence of this idea of recapitulation, Irenaeus maintained that Jesus was 49 when he was crucified, the age when one 'declines into seniority'. All human experience, even old age, is thus 'recapitulated' and set right in Jesus' earthly life. The doctrine extends into eschatology. After the resurrection, Irenaeus is clear that there will be a period where the righteous, in their resurrected flesh, will rule over a restored version of the present creation, setting right the present unsatisfactory state of affairs.

Irenaeus' absolute conviction that the Father of Jesus Christ is the creator spoken of in the OT is at one with his insistence on the reality of the Incarnation. He relies heavily on the prologue to John's gospel for its teaching that Christ as Word coexisted with the Father, definitively differentiating him from any Gnostic emanation. The Word took on real human flesh and this is guaranteed by the transformation of the humble elements of bread and wine into Christ's body in the eucharist. All these doctrines interact to shape his understanding of the positive relationship between the material and spiritual universe and allow him to defend the bodily resurrection with vigour. Indeed the analogy of the eucharist provides him with one of his strongest arguments. If bread and wine could become the body of Christ and so be both earthly and heavenly, earthly human bodies nourished by the eucharistic elements could also have a heavenly, incorruptible aspect.

In the process, Irenaeus also expands on the analogy that Justin Martyr had already drawn between Eve and Mary. As a woman's disobedience gave rise to the fall, so a woman's obedience leads to the incarnation. Here too, the common Gnostic condemnation of woman and particularly childbirth as the deplorable device which perpetuates the entrapment of spirit in matter is confuted. The analogy goes so far as his characterization of Mary as the 'womb of humanity'. As we are all Eve's children, so through the incarnation every Christian is Mary's child. Irenaeus thus has a place in the developing understanding of Mary's significance in orthodox thought.

This idea of recapitulation is a powerful soteriological image. It also becomes for Irenaeus a further proof of the identity of the Father with the Creator. Only if the Father of Christ and the creator of Adam were the same could this plan of salvation work. It has left a problematic heritage in other ways, however. For instance, there are difficulties in understanding how Jesus recapitulates the experience of women, whose lives he did not retrace, and whom Irenaeus certainly never mentions in this regard. The notion of Jesus as encapsulating all human experience can detract from his specific Jewish, 1st-century identity and underlies continuing theological debates about the ordination of women, for instance.

Irenaeus ties his theology to the guaranteed authority of the apostolic succession of bishops, giving shape to the formidable ecclesiology which has sustained the institutional church throughout the centuries. It has also only too often tempted the church to regard institutional structures and their survival as its priority at the cost of the freedom of the Spirit. There can be no doubt that the history of Western Christianity in particular has been profoundly shaped by his legacy. Later thinkers may expand on or contradict his ideas, but his fundamental conviction of the coherence of Christian teaching around the incarnation is the premiss on which subsequent Christian thought is based.

Grant, R. M., *Irenaeus of Lyons* (1997).

Minns, D., *Irenaeus* (1994).

Nielsen, J. T., *Adam and Christ in the Theology of Irenaeus of Lyons* (1968).

Origen (185–c.254)

HENRI CROUZEL

Origen was born, probably at Alexandria, of Christian parents. The education given him by his father Leonides (martyred when Origen was 17) was both Hellenistic and biblical. Origen taught 'grammar' (i.e. literature) and was appointed head of the school of catechetics while still very young. For the first part of his life, to 231, he taught in his native city, but after his ordination as priest at Caesarea in Palestine, Bishop Demetrius' hostility compelled him to leave Alexandria for Caesarea. Here he reopened his school, about which we have abundant evidence from a eulogy by one of his students, the future Gregory Thaumaturgus. He was imprisoned and tortured during Decius' persecution and died about 254 from the after-effects, probably at Tyre, where his tomb in the cathedral was to be seen in the 13th century.

Thanks to one of his Alexandrian converts, Ambrose, who used his wealth to maintain a secretariat and copyists' workshop, Origen left a vast body of work, which survives only partially. Heading the list is the *Hexapla*, a titanic collaborative production on which he worked throughout his life. He set out in six columns (eight or even nine for some books) the entire OT as follows: the Hebrew in Hebrew letters;

the Hebrew in Greek letters; the Greek versions of Aquila, Symmachus, the Septuagint (the official Christian text), and Theodotion; plus, for some books, supplementary versions designated Quinta, Sexta, and possibly Septima. Special signs (asterisk and obelus) marked places where the Septuagint had more or less text than others, probably to facilitate Jewish–Christian dialogue by indicating what was or was not accepted by the other party. The last complete edition of the surviving fragments is Field's (1867; 1870; 1960) but many other fragments have since come to light. Because of the controversies after his death and Justinian's systematic destruction of his manuscripts, most of Origen's work is lost in the original Greek, though some survives in Latin translations by Rufinus of Aquileia, Jerome, and an unknown translator.

Most of his work is exegetical. We still have in Greek a few books of his *Commentary on John*, possibly his *chef-d'œuvre*, and of his *Commentary on Matthew*, some of which were translated into Latin by an unknown 5th-century writer. Rufinus has left abridged Latin versions of the *Commentary on Romans* and the *Commentary on the Song of Songs*, an early masterpiece of mystical writing. There are also nearly three hundred homilies on the scriptures, a score (on Jeremiah) surviving in Greek, the others in Latin.

A few non-exegetical works survive: *On First Principles* (*Peri archon*), a first attempt at a synthesis of the Christian faith, complete in Rufinus' Latin translation, one-seventh in Greek; *Contra Celsum*, a refutation of a Platonic philosopher and the most significant of the Apologies, in Greek; also in Greek, two little treatises on prayer and martyrdom. We also have two collections of quotations, the *Apologia of Origen* by the martyr Pamphilus in Rufinus' Latin, and the *Philocalia of Origen*, in Greek, attributed to Basil of Caesarea and Gregory Nazianzen.

Origen is an indissoluble combination of exegete, master of spirituality, and speculative theologian; seeing only one of these aspects risks serious distortion. He tends to be seen chiefly as an allegorizer, whereas he is one of the great literal exegetes of his time. He investigates different readings in the manuscripts and usually explains the literal meaning before allegorizing. His frequent statement that such-and-such a passage has no valid literal sense has been misunderstood: for him the literal sense did not mean what was intended by the author, but just the actual words, the author's intention being included in the spiritual sense. He means that figurative language has no valid literal meaning. He actually values the literal sense more highly than the most conservative modern exegetes, as witness his defence of the historicity of Noah's Ark against the Marcionite Apelles.

But the literal sense veils a spiritual or allegorical sense intended by God. The whole OT is a prophecy of the New, which in turn is a participation in the 'eternal Gospel' of beatitude: such is the intention of the Spirit inspiring the scriptures. All scripture bears a spiritual sense, which the believer must discover on reading. All was written with this intention for us Christians (1 Cor. 10: 11), including the OT, which thus reveals its meaning, as at the Transfiguration Moses and Elijah, symbolizing the law and the prophets, shine with the light of the transfigured Christ. The OT is revelation only because it is all a prophecy of Christ, while the NT allows us to apply what is said of Christ to the Christian. The 'eternal Gospel' of the state of beatitude will convey, 'face to face', in all their fullness the realities which the 'temporal Gospel', here below, has shown 'in a mirror, as enigma' (1 Cor. 13: 12), but nevertheless as realities, whereas the OT gave us only the 'shadow' of them, not, like the New, a real participation.

Origen is always, in all his exegesis, a master of spirituality. According to his anthropology, human beings consist of spirit (*pneuma*), soul (*psyche*), and body (*soma*). The 'spirit which is in man' is a participation in the Holy Spirit: it is the pedagogue of the soul, which becomes spiritual in proportion to its assimilation to the spirit. But if the soul surrenders to the flesh (*sarx*), thus assimilating itself to the body, it becomes instead wholly carnal. Thus the soul is both the arena and the prize of the spiritual combat.

Starting from scripture, Origen created a number of themes that recur in mystical literature. Thus the Bride in the Song of Songs, besides the traditional collective interpretation as the church, bears an individual meaning as the Christian soul, the bride of Christ through membership of the bride-church. The Christian life is the birth and growth of Christ in the soul: if Christ is not born in each one of us, his birth at Bethlehem has no meaning for us. The ascent of the three apostles to the Mount of Transfiguration signifies the ascetical striving that prepares the soul for the vision of God, with no encroachment on God's absolute freedom. The five spiritual senses, by analogy with the five bodily senses, represent the possibility of an intuitive knowledge of God, by a connaturality revealed as humanity participates progressively in the image of God, that is, his Son, to the point of perfection, the 'likeness' of beatitude. Origen has a comprehensive doctrine of the knowledge of God and identifies it with the union of love, quoting Gen. 4: 1, 'Adam knew Eve, his wife': knowledge and love are one thing. His too is the theme of the shaft and wound of love, combining Isa. 49: 2, where the Servant of Yahweh (Christ) says of God, 'He has made me a sharp arrow, hidden me in his quiver', with Song of Songs 2: 5, where the Bride says 'I am sick with love'. There are some testimonies in his work to a personal mystical experience (rare, because he says very little about himself), leading Henri de Lubac to call him 'one of the greatest mystics of the Christian tradition'.

Finally, Origen is a great theologian, Augustine and Aquinas his only peers in Christian history. His theology has been seriously misunderstood, leading to his being unjustly branded a heretic. He has not been judged on his work as a whole, nor even on what remains of it; his accusers have lacked historical sense, not seeing him in the context of his time nor taking the trouble to explain one passage by reference to another in some other work, or even sometimes in the same one. Their excuse, apart from the sheer volume of his work, must be that he was not concerned to 'define' his thought, i.e. to state it with all the nuances and antitheses to be found in other writings. This concern hardly existed for the church fathers of the first three centuries: it arose later under the combined influence of Roman law and controversy with the Arians, who were good at discovering their own doctrines in their adversaries' statements. Origen's is a theology 'in process of research'— he himself says 'in training'—rather than something finished and elaborated.

One of his main preoccupations was with the numerous heresies, Gnostic and other, of his time. Against the Marcionites he affirmed the goodness of the creator, his identity with the Father of Jesus, the agreement of the two Testaments and the value of the Old; against the Valentinians, free will, personal responsibility, rejection of any predestination arising from differences in human nature; against the modalists, the distinct personality of each of the divine persons; against the adoptionists, the eternal generation of the Word; against the Docetists, the real humanity of Christ. He also combated some tendencies within the Church—anthropomorphists, millenarianists, and literalists against whom he affirmed the incorporeal nature of God, the soul, and beatitude, and Christ's abolition of the letter of the Jewish Law.

The philosophical basis of Origen's thought is a moderate Platonism mixed with Stoicism and a touch of Aristotelianism, as appears from Gregory Thaumaturgus' account of his teaching. But he cannot be called a philosopher, what he drew from these sources being wholly in the service of theology.

He expresses the unity of the divine persons and the personality proper to each dynamically rather than ontologically. The generation of the Son by the Father is both eternal and, from our human point of view, continual; the Spirit derives from the Father through the Son. The Son remains forever in the Father, even when here on earth with his human soul. The statement that 'there is no moment when he (the Son) was not', which occurs three times in Origen's works (*Peri archon*, 1. 2. 9; 4. 4. 1; *Com. Rom.* 1. 5) cannot, as some have suggested, be inauthentic, for the second passage was quoted by Athanasius (*De doctrina Nicaenae synodi*, 27. 1–2), and explicitly attributed to Origen. The generation of the Son does not imply a division of the Father's substance— *probole*, Latin *prolatio*—as in the doctrine Origen attributes to the Valentinians. The 'subordinationism' with which he is frequently reproached is simply the affirmation that the Father is primary, being the origin of the others and giving them their missions, with no implication of superiority of nature.

The heart of Origen's christology is his doctrine of the titles (*epinoiai*) of the Son—the different names he is given in scripture, by allegorical exegesis in the OT, directly in the NT. They correspond to his different activities relating to humanity and creation. Origen details about a hundred, the two most important being Wisdom and Word. As Wisdom the Son is the Intelligible World, containing the seeds and principles of all beings, the mysteries corresponding to the Platonic world of ideas; as Word he is the revealer of the mysteries and the agent of creation. In accordance with Origen's doctrine of the pre-existence of souls, called in this context 'intelligences', the soul of Christ was created with the others, not from all eternity, but from the moment of its creation it was united to the Word and was thus 'in the form of God'. This soul was the spouse of the church, i.e. of the totality of the other intelligences, but it alone did not sin, as the others did to varying degrees. Their Fall is seen as a diminishing in fervour or a wearying of beatitude, something like the 'acedia' described by the Greek monks. The varying depth of this Fall divided the pre-existing intelligences into angels, men, and demons. They all had ethereal bodies hitherto, but after the Fall those becoming humans took on a terrestrial quality so that they would be in a state of testing, enabling them to redeem their fault. The pre-existing intelligence of Christ also assumed a carnal body, without having sinned, in order to rejoin his fallen spouse, the

pre-existing church now fallen into flesh. The OT is like a time of be-
trothal during which Christ has not yet revealed himself to the spouse,
the OT church. In the NT, he has been reunited with his spouse, but this
is not yet perfect union, which will be for the end of time.

Thus Christ became incarnate in Mary to redeem his fallen spouse
and reveal divinity to her. During the Passion his human soul was
handed over in ransom to Satan who, not recognizing the bond between
Christ and God, took it down to Hades, where it liberated the souls
held captive and took them with it in its Ascension. This is how Origen
teaches the hypostatic union (for the Word is always with his human
soul while still always with the Father) and introduces the concept of
the 'communication of idioms' between the Word and the human soul
united to him (whereby what is said of the one can be predicated also of
the other).

Humanity, like the angels, was created according to the image of
God, which is the Word, and participates in the existence and divinity of
the Father and the sonship and rationality of the Word. But sin covers
over the image of God in humanity with other images, diabolical or
bestial, which only the Redeemer can remove. As regards risen bodies,
Origen affirms both their identity with and their difference from terrestrial bodies, invoking the Pauline simile of seed and plant (1 Cor. 15:
34–44), in using which he is practically unique at this early period. He
does not regard Mary as exempt from all sin, but he is the first to affirm,
explicitly, her perpetual virginity, implicit in Justin and Irenaeus. He
sees her as a great exemplar of the spiritual life, and, according to the
historian Socrates (*Church History*, 7. 32), he called her *Theotokos*,
Mother of God. He gives precise teaching on five of the seven sacraments (not confirmation or anointing of the sick).

The pre-existence of souls seems to be Origen's only demonstrable
'heresy', which cannot be called heresy in his time, for the church had
no teaching on the matter. His vision of *apocatastasis*, i.e. restoration
at the end of time, derived from 1 Cor. 15: 23–6, is not pantheistic. As

for the salvation of the devil, he has left contradictory texts, the clearest denial being in his *Letter to Friends in Alexandria*, quoted by both Rufinus and Jerome at the height of their quarrel, and thus, despite being in Latin, difficult to dispute. Other errors with which he is reproached arise from misunderstandings, or from later specialization of terminology.

Attacks on Origen, based on misunderstandings, began soon after his death, for example the two attacks of Methodius of Olympus, at the turn of the 3rd and 4th centuries, about the glorified body and the eternity of the world. These attacks were answered in the *Apologia of Origen* by the martyr Pamphilus of Caesarea, who explained the texts in question by reference to others in Origen's works. The great Doctors of the 4th century are all to a greater or lesser extent his disciples. But Jerome, starting as a fervent Origenist, turned against him after 393 and attacked him in argument with his old friend Rufinus. In the 6th century the Emperor Justinian entered the fray, condemning Origen as interpreted by contemporary 'Origenists', first in a local council in 543, then in a council held some time before the fifth Ecumenical (Constantinople II); this second council is clearly directed against contemporary Origenists. These attacks were made by men lacking in philosophical and theological understanding, but most of all in historical sense, unaware of the change in mentality between the small, persecuted church of Origen's time and the triumphant church of their own. They accuse him in terms of the heresies of their time, not those that he himself faced and that dictated his line of argument. They were unaware of the theological advance stimulated by the Arian crisis, and even of changes in terminology. They projected the 'Origenism' of their time on to Origen, did not explain difficult passages by reference to others, made no distinction between Origen writing 'by way of exploration' and Origen as teacher, and finally judged him by a conception of orthodoxy increasingly dependent on Roman law. Hence their case against him is without validity.

Ever since the 15th century, with Pico della Mirandola and Erasmus, Origen has been a subject of serious study, but in the second half of the 20th century interest in him grew among a large number of scholars. Their four-yearly congress brings together as many as 120 people from several European and American countries, and from Japan. After Augustine, Origen is probably at present the most studied of all the church fathers. Now that more exact historical work has revealed his true greatness, unconfused by any later 'Origenism', it seems that his 'exploratory theology', with its basis in scripture and its inspiration drawn from spiritual experience, corresponds very closely to the aspirations of our own age.

Origen, *Commentary on Matthew, Books I, II, X–XIV*, ed. J. Patrick (1897).

—— *The Philocalia*, ed. G. Lewis (1911).

—— *Prayer; Exhortation to Martyrdom*, ed. J. J. O'Meara (1954).

—— *The Song of Songs, Commentary and Homilies*, ed. R. Lawson (1957).

—— *On First Principles*, ed. B. W. Butterworth, 2nd edn. (1966).

—— *Contra Celsum*, ed. H. Chadwick, 3rd edn. (1979).

—— *Homilies on Genesis and Exodus*, ed. R. Heine (1982).

—— *Commentary on the Gospel According to John, Books 1–10*, ed. R. Heine (1989); *Books 13–32* (1993).

—— *Homilies on Leviticus 1–16*, ed. G. W. Barkley (1990).

—— *Treatises on the Passover; Dialogue with Heraclides and his Fellow Bishops on the Father, the Son and the Soul*, ed. R. J. Daly (1992).

—— *Homilies on Luke; Fragments on Luke*, ed. J. T. Lienhard (1996).

Bigg, C., *The Christian Platonists of Alexandria* (1913).

Crouzel, H., *Origen* (1984), ET (1989).

—— *Bibliographie critique d'Origène*, with Supplements I and II (1996).

Daniélou, J., *Origen* (1948), ET (1955).

Drewery, B., *Origen and the Doctrine of Grace* (1960).

Hanson, R., *Origen's Doctrine of Tradition* (1954).

—— *Allegory and Event* (1959).

Westcott, B. F., 'Origen and the Beginnings of Christian Philosophy', in *Essays on the History of Religious Thought in the West* (1891).

Athanasius (298/9–373)

CHARLES KANNENGIESSER

We know little of Athanasius' early years. He records no personal experience of the fierce persecution by Diocletian in his home town, Alexandria, which continued until he was about 14 years of age. That he was well educated is clear from his later writings, impregnated with the bible and the works of earlier Christian teachers such as Origen.

Athanasius went with Bishop Alexander to the Council of Nicaea in 325 as a deacon and secretary and in the summer of 328 was elected to succeed Alexander and so continue his struggle against Arianism. He was not yet 30 years of age, young enough to give episcopal opponents a convenient pretext for invalidating his nomination. In 335, Emperor Constantine exiled him to Trier, or, as Athanasius himself would have said, 'to the end of the world', from where he returned two years later, after Constantine's death, only to be deposed again in 339. This time he found refuge in Rome, welcomed by Pope Julius I. Back home at length in 346, he enjoyed ten relatively quiet years. Military power, combined with the relentless hostility of some bishops, forced him to flee again in 356, this time into hiding for six years among the monastic settlements of Egypt's deserts. A fourth and fifth exile of shorter length followed, but Athanasius had outlived all his enemies, becoming in old age a living legend, the most authoritative voice of the Nicene form of orthodoxy, according to the praise expressed by such younger contemporaries as Basil of Caesarea.

Athanasius never posed as an intellectual of high learning, comparable to Origen or Eusebius of Caesarea. He was born for pastoral action, able to perceive with an independent mind the new opportunities given to the church by the turn of events linked with Constantine's government. His swift reactions and adamant convictions not only demonstrated his natural authority, but generated enduring friendships in the places he visited. From each of his forced exiles his returns to Alexandria gained popular acclaim. On the other hand, he was the most targeted church official of his time, remaining for over two decades under direct attack by a large fraction of the eastern bishops led by the court favourite, Eusebius of Nicomedia, and opposed in his own diocese by a dissident group of clergy and monks.

Best known as the defender of Nicaea, Athanasius contributed more than anyone else to the structuring of an anti-Arian form of orthodox faith. How he did it reveals the true genius of his personal assimilation of the bible. The youthful deacon of 325, called three years later to the episcopal office, had to spend much time during his first five years as a bishop performing pastoral visitations of local churches under his jurisdiction and of monastic groups spread over various desert regions of Egypt and Libya. In the meantime ecclesiastical politics were building up a menacing offensive against the see of Alexandria, with the declared intention of rehabilitating Arius whose condemnation for heresy had been confirmed at Nicaea by imperial power. By the time Athanasius had completed his prolonged retreats among the monks, he had forged a vision of his own, free from political concerns, but capable of rallying a majority of believers under his leadership. He wrote that vision down in an essay entitled *On the Incarnation of the Divine Logos*.

On the Incarnation is a work of matured pastoral experience engaging in a fundamental rethinking of the theological trends derived from Origen's legacy inside the Alexandrian church, precisely where the heresy of Arius had originated. By a deliberate remodelling of Origen's doctrine of salvation, Athanasius placed the Incarnation of the Word (Logos) centre stage in the world drama of divine redemption. He could not have demonstrated more effectively, against Arianism, the proper divinity of the Logos than by showing that no one less than God himself could, as saviour, effect the divinization of humanity. The aim was not political (when he wrote it he was, unknowingly, on the eve of his first exile), but the truly pastoral and non-polemical thesis of *On the Incarnation* laid the foundation of the incarnational theology that was to prevail in ancient Christianity through the Cappadocian Fathers in the east, Ambrose and Augustine in the west. Into the theoretical framework of divine revelation and salvific knowledge inherited from Origen, Athanasius introduced a massive array of quotations from Pauline letters focusing on the dialectic of life and death in Christ's mystery (*On the Incarnation*, 8–11), which gave a 'physical' connotation to the traditional idea of the divinizing transformation of human beings.

In exile at Trier or shortly afterwards, Athanasius waded into the fray of the post-Nicene controversy by composing his most important doctrinal exposition, the *Orations against the Arians*. A dating around 340 makes it possible to compare the *Orations* and the many pamphlets, letters, and dogmatic statements issued by the bishop during the next three decades of his long career. The comparison demonstrates the prime value of the *Orations* in the mind of their author, who never tired of multiplying doctrinal variations based on them, the most striking example being the *Letters to Serapion on the Divinity of the Spirit*, written in the late 350s. Orations 1 and 2 (3 may be from another hand) provide a strong articulation of baptismal faith in the divine Trinity with central attention given to the substantial relation between Father and Son in line with the Creed of Nicaea (one notes that the author never uses the hotly controverted Nicene *homoousios* as part of his own theological vocabulary).

Once more Athanasius updated Origen's thought. By contemplating the Trinity in the concrete light of the gospel-event, instead of speculating—in reference to Father and Son—on the nature of the human psyche and its capacity to know divine mysteries, Athanasius succeeded in teaching a consistent theory about the inner life of the three Hypostases, a term Origen had been the first to use in this connection. By playing with the analogy between saved and saviour, Athanasius juxtaposed the experienced reality of baptismal rebirth with the image of the Son in the 'bosom' of the Father (John 1: 18). Thus, the conclusion of the Johannine prologue became as central for Athanasius' thought as the prologue's initial verses had been for Origen when composing his *Commentary on John*.

Athanasius deepened his anti-Arian position over the years. Much that he wrote was strongly polemical and political but it needs stressing that his political involvement in the imperial scene was from the start *imposed* on him, as was the repeated duress and physical violence against his people. Against his will, Athanasius was kept for over a quarter of a century at the core of a conflict in which political ambitions and theological principles collided. It is no surprise if his writings dating from the 350s and 360s consist mainly in polemical apologies and letters. A distinctive feature of these writings, produced in self-defence, is their documentary exactness; another is the obsessive denunciation by the beleaguered pontiff of all his adversaries as 'Arians'. A welcome diversion from the endless controversies is provided by the synod of Alexandria, 362, a synod for union and reconciliation, the first of its kind, organized by Athanasius with the purpose of harmonizing the doctrinal positions of different pro-Nicene schools of thought.

A more serene image of Athanasius irradiates his pastoral and spiritual writings in which his deeper self finds its genuine expression. Recent hostile historiography has systematically ignored such testimonies, or even denied his authorship of them, as in the case of the *Life of Antony*, without any philological or historical grounds.

The *Festal Letters*, composed each year months in advance by the bishop to announce the dates of Lent, Easter, and Pentecost, are the most original of his pastoral productions. Athanasius transformed the genre of these circular letters, giving them a popular and homiletic twist. In their vibrant exhortations the church leader vanishes behind the spiritual adviser. Through them, as through his influential *Letter to Marcellinus on the Psalms*, the pastor dispensed the biblical riches of his personal culture.

The *Life of Antony* reveals an author perfectly conscious of his composition and purpose, eager to produce a paradigmatic work rich in spiritual significance, but keeping the narrative close to down-to-earth reality. Antony the Hermit, already venerated in his lifetime as an icon and a model by the numerous solitaries who populated the deserts of Egypt from the end of the 3rd century, died in 356. It is probable that Athanasius visited him in the early years of his tenure, and at least once Antony made the trip to Alexandria in support of Athanasius' cause. Before his death Antony bequeathed his only cloak to Athanasius. In the *Life of Antony*, written shortly after 356, the 'Father of all monks' takes on a paradigmatic format, his struggle with the demons inspiring many painters and novelists through the centuries up to the present day. Antony's speeches to audiences of pagan philosophers, Christian ascetics, bureaucrats of the imperial administration, or Alexandrian clergy show rhetorical skills and establish a line of orthodox thought so precisely conformed to Athanasius' own thinking that we cannot but hear the latter speaking through the deceased hermit. The *Life* was destined to become the first Christian best-seller after the bible.

In a global evaluation of Christian thought, as it structured itself through antiquity, the Middle Ages, and modernity, the contribution of Athanasius remains considerable and a painstaking retrieval of his legacy has a special urgency in a time of fundamental doctrinal shifts.

To recapitulate: a central aspect of that contribution is the bishop's own *hermeneutical* approach towards scripture; a second essential feature is his *political* consciousness. His lifelong struggle exemplifies for the first time in Christian history what it means for the church at large to give Caesar and God their proper due. Thirdly, as an intellectual leader engaged in pastoral ministry, the 4th-century 'pope' of Alexandria showed a *theological* capacity to reformulate the Christian message according to the needs of the church in his time, authoritatively interpreting Nicene orthodoxy for both east and west. Fourthly, Athanasius, a man of the common touch, spontaneously took the lead in the most popular religious revival of his own time, the monastic movement. Long before any other Christian hierarch, he acted in solidarity on *mystical* ground with solitaries and communities, male and female, addressing to them most of his writings.

A man of the bible who wrote no biblical commentaries, Athanasius posthumously 'lent' his name to such exegetical works composed by pious but one-sided admirers. The 'Athanasian Creed', written in his name by a Latin author of the 5th century, reached a quasi-canonical status in western Christianity. His genuine teaching on God's incarnation was to remain seriously vitiated up to the present time by pseudo-Athanasian writings. The discovery of the authentic Athanasius remains a challenge for the historian of Christian thought.

Arnold, D. W. H., *The Episcopal Career of Athanasius of Alexandria* (1991).

Barnes, T. D., *Athanasius and Constantius* (1993).

Brakke, D., *Athanasius and the Politics of Asceticism* (1995).

Bright, P. (trans.), 'Letter to Marcellinus', in C. Kannengiesser (ed.), *Early Christian Spirituality* (1986).

Gregg, R. C., *Athanasius: Life of Antony and Letter to Marcellinus* (1980).

Grillmeier, A. I., *Christ in Christian Tradition*, 2nd edn. (1975).

Hanson, R. P. C., *The Search for the Christian Doctrine of God* (1988).

Kannengiesser, C., *Arius and Alexander: Two Alexandrian Theologians* (1991).

—— 'Athanasius of Alexandria and the Ascetic Movement of his Time', in V. L. Wimbush and R. Valantasis (eds.), *Asceticism* (1995).

Robertson, A., *Saint Athanasius, Select Works and Letters* (1891; repr. 1952; 1987).

Thomson, R. W., *Contra Gentes and De Incarnatione* (1980).

Widdicombe, P., *The Fatherhood of God from Origen to Athanasius* (1994).

Augustine (353–430)

CAROL HARRISON

Aurelius Augustine, bishop of Hippo, stands at a watershed in the history of western thought, between the classical world of the Roman empire and the Middle Ages.

Born into a family of minor gentry in the small inland town of Thagaste (modern Souk Arras) in Roman North Africa, son of Monica, a Christian, whom he was to make one of the most famous mothers of history, and Patrick, a Roman citizen, pagan, but converted to Christianity near the end of his life, Augustine enjoyed the distinctive, privileged education which identified and formed the ruling class of the empire. Thus he entered an aristocracy not of birth but of educational formation. At the school of grammar at Thagaste, and then, thanks to a wealthy patron, the schools of rhetoric at Madaura and Carthage, Augustine was introduced to the intricacies of textual, grammatical study of the classic authors (Cicero, Virgil, Sallust, Terence), and of the disciplines of the liberal arts which reached their goal in the formation of the rhetor—a man practised in the art of teaching, moving, and persuading his audience by eloquence. Augustine exercised his chosen profession, as a teacher of rhetoric, at Carthage (376–83),

Rome (383–4), and then at Milan (384–6), the imperial capital, where, in the municipal chair of rhetoric, he had the ear of the emperor. He might not unreasonably have hoped for advancement to a provincial governorship. Instead, in 386, he converted to Christianity.

Faith and reason 🌿

Augustine's *Confessions*, which he began to write ten years later as a bishop, provide us with a retrospective interpretation of the events which led to his conversion (books 1–8). They read as if Augustine was never not a Christian: it is the religion to which he had been born, which he had drunk in with his mother's milk; the religion to which he had been dedicated as a child and from which he had strayed. He rejected Cicero's *Hortensius*, or *Exhortation to Philosophy*, which he read in the course of his studies, aged 19, because, although it fired him with a burning desire to find wisdom, 'the name of Christ was not there'. Instead, having briefly examined the Christian scriptures and found them to be rather crudely written for his rhetor's taste, he turned to the Manichees, a religious sect based on revelations given to the prophet Mani (b. 216 AD), characterized by its universal, missionary purpose and its syncretistic, dualistic, cosmological myths. The Manichees claimed to possess truth and to present a rational explanation of the universe, evil, the soul, and salvation. This, together with their impressive literature, asceticism, communal life, the fact that they criticized precisely those aspects of Christianity that Augustine himself found offputting (the emphasis upon faith, anthropomorphic ideas of God, inconsistencies in scripture), and above all their claim to represent true Christianity, to be *integri Christiani*, perhaps explains why Augustine remained with them for the next nine years. His enthusiasm was undermined by a growing realization that their claim to truth was no more than pseudo-science, that in fact they did not have the answers; most especially, their dualistic theory of evil raised insuperable problems in relation to the omnipotence and sovereignty of God. Moreover, their much-vaunted asceticism proved to be a matter more of theory than of practice.

Augustine temporarily despaired of ever finding 'wisdom', and extracted himself from the alluring scepticism of the New Academy only by acknowledging that he could not find the 'saving name of Christ' there. Instead he became a catechumen, one undergoing instruction for baptism in the Catholic Church, following the 'precedent of [his] parents' and while waiting for a 'clear light' to determine his path. The light was to come from two directions, first from Ambrose, bishop of Milan, whose preaching delighted Augustine not only in its eloquence but because his spiritual interpretation enabled him to overcome the problems that the Manichees' literal, rational approach had highlighted. The second direction was from the philosophy termed 'Neoplatonism' which was being studied and discussed by various individuals at Milan. From one of them he came across some 'books of the Platonists' (Augustine's vagueness is tantalizing and deliberate— probably some Plotinus, an Egyptian Greek who taught at Rome, author of the *Enneads*, and maybe some Porphyry, Plotinus' disciple and editor). The revolutionary thing about the Neoplatonists was their teaching that true reality was spiritual. This insight enabled Augustine to break free of the materialism which the Manichees shared with many of the philosophers of the day, from difficult, physical conceptions of God, and gave him an alternative to the Manichees' dualistic explanation of evil as inherent in matter. Rather, he was able to follow Plotinus in teaching the initiative of the good in giving form to matter, and evil as a declining from this order whilst being comprehended by it— a sort of *privatio boni* (privation of the good) which Augustine attributed, in man, to the free will.

The 'books of the Platonists' also allowed Augustine to 'return into' (*Ennead*, 5. 1) himself, to appreciate himself as a spiritual being; to find God, true Being, as the foundation of himself, within, and to realize that God transcends him: 'more inward than my inmost being and higher than my highest'. Numerous passages that describe an ascent towards God have prompted some scholars to speak of Augustine's 'spirituality' or 'mysticism', and to evaluate how much this owes to Neoplatonism—for they are undeniably Neoplatonic in form (introversion, ascent from the material world, to the soul, to the mind, and above the mind to God). But Augustine's emphasis on divine initiative and help, and his later emphasis on the need for a mediator, give them a definite Christian colouring. Augustine's later attitude to the Platonists is determined by his doctrine of the Fall and of Christ's saving work: it is summed up in his observation that, although the philosophers may see the goal, the homeland, the truth, they do not follow the way to it, and will therefore never attain it, for the only way is the way of the cross (*Tractates on John*, 28. 5), made possible by Christ the One Mediator (*Letter*, 118; *City of God*, 9–10 (against pagan theurgy); *On the Trinity*, 4. 13). Their presumption and pride are contrasted with Christian confession and humility, their confidence in reason, like that of the Manichees, with Christian faith in authority, as the only way to attain truth.

The will 🌿

Thus, at least on the basis of the *Confessions*, it might be argued that Augustine was simply reconciling himself to Christianity. But this was not merely an intellectual reconciliation, it was also a matter for the will. *Confessions* 1–8 paint a vivid picture of the vitiated and flawed nature of the human will, divided against, and alienated from, itself; willing the good but unable to do it. This was a matter of personal experience (he could not give up his sexual relations with women and embrace the chastity which, for him, was inseparable from conversion) which Augustine found confirmed by Paul, whose admonitions in Rom. 13: 13–14 were to precipitate his famous conversion in the garden at Milan (*Confessions*, 8).

Augustine's portrait of the vitiated will is not just retrospective interpretation of what he experienced before conversion, but is rather the result of sustained reflection upon the fallen nature of the human will even after conversion. This is first evidenced in a series of works he wrote on Paul, and especially Romans, during the 390s and which culminate in *To Simplicianus*, with its uncompromising teaching on the fallenness of man: the Fall of Adam, humankind as a *massa peccati*, 'one lump in which the original guilt [of Adam] remains throughout' (*Simpl.* 2. 17, 20), the culpability of all, the impotence of the will to do the good, the unmerited grace of God which can alone (and regardless of faith, reason, or works) inspire a delight in the good. Whilst a doctrine of original sin was not unknown in African theology, this work, with its application of the Fall to the human will, marks a crucial break with the classical ethical tradition, which tended to uphold humanity's moral and intellectual autonomy, and the attainability of perfection in this life. It also foreshadows his later controversy with the Pelagians (415 onwards), who represented this late antique viewpoint to their ascetic followers in theological arguments against original sin and the necessity of infant baptism and in support of the freedom of the will and the possibility of sinlessness by rational observance of the law. In numerous works to counter these propositions (especially as voiced by Julian of Eclanum, against whom he wrote until his death) Augustine emphasized the double commandment of love of God and neighbour as the standard of virtue: a love inspired by God's gracious gift of his Holy Spirit (Rom. 5: 5) and without which man is simply free to sin. The will is only free in acknowledging its dependence upon God's gracious inspiration, which enables it to delight in and to do the good, and to love in accordance with the true order of reality under God. The logical outworking of his theology of the Fall, original sin, and grace was an uncompromising doctrine of election and predestination which, for his critics (the monks at Hadrumetum and of southern Gaul), left no room for human initiative or responsibility, but for Augustine expressed the wholly unmerited and gratuitous nature of salvation in circumstances where all justly deserve damnation. Why some are saved and some left to perish he attributed to the unfathomable wisdom of God (Rom. 11: 33). Augustinian realism (or, some would have it, pessimism) as opposed to Pelagian optimism (or, some would have it, realism) and ideas of perfectibility, have been re-expressed in countless different forms in the history of western theology and, as Iris Murdoch (*Sovereignty of the Good*, 1970) forcefully demonstrated, are still manifest in secular philosophical attitudes following the Enlightenment.

Christian society ✍

For Augustine the Christian life is a social life, a community of people with 'one heart and one mind' towards God (Acts 4: 32). He was convinced that this single-minded devotion was best preserved by chastity (which for him was as much a matter of the mind as the body). From the 'philosophical' retreat with family and friends at Cassiciacum, immediately following his conversion (386), to the lay, celibate, community of 'servants of God' which he established at Thagaste on his return to Africa (388), to the lay and then clerical monastery which he established next to the basilica at Hippo following his ordination as priest (391) and consecration as bishop (396/7) respectively, Augustine aimed to establish a community of like-minded individuals with whom he could live the Christian life. The emphasis (as evidenced in *The Rule* and *On Virginity*) in Augustine's monasticism is not so much ascetic as upon common life, sharing of goods, friendship, and brotherly love—reflecting a theology in which pride and self-love are the cause of the Fall, and love of God and neighbour are the source, means, and end of grace. This has, not unjustly, been termed a 'spiritual communism', and is the basis for Augustinian communities throughout the world today.

Augustine does not set the married life in antithesis to the monastic life, rather he sees it as sharing the same ideals, goals, and temporal ambiguities. The married relationship is defined not so much by the sexual bond (this is simply part of the 'friendly fellowship' of marriage and of the duty which spouses owe to one another regardless of procreation) as by unity, harmony, and fidelity; a marriage of minds rather than of bodies. Alone among theologians of late antiquity (with the exception of Ambrosiaster) he entertains the possibility of sexual relations before the Fall and maintains that Adam and Eve were a married couple. The nature of human sexuality after the Fall comes to prominence in the later debates with Julian on the nature of concupiscence— the violent and irrational carnal feeling which is symptomatic of the disobedient, disordered will following the Fall, and which accompanies the transmission of Adam's sin. Augustine's positive reflections on marriage and sexuality as part of humanity's original creation are often ignored by those who simply wish to regard him as the *eminence grise* of western negative attitudes.

Both the monastic and the married life therefore anticipate for Augustine the perfect community of unity, mutual love, and friendship which will be the City of God, but neither, because of man's fallenness, can realize it in this life. Nor, unlike the Donatists, did he think it could be attained in the church.

An inordinately large part of Augustine's time and energy as a bishop was consumed by attempts to wipe out the schismatic church of the Donatists which had become so deeply entrenched in North Africa through its claim to have preserved the true church, pure and untainted by the compromise and corruption which, they alleged, had vitiated the Catholic Church during the persecutions. Sermons, treatises, letters, public debate, even a popular song, were used by Augustine to demonstrate the absurdity of the Donatists' position in setting themselves not only against the Catholic Church in Africa but against the universal church. The ecclesiology and sacramental theology expounded in this context has been determinative of the western church ever since. Both sides appealed to African tradition, notably Cyprian, bishop of Carthage, and to the state, to support their position. All else having failed, the Donatists were effectively coerced into defeat by a harsh series of proscriptions in 412 which, in a number of works, Augustine seems to have argued himself into supporting.

The unattainability of perfection in this life is described in world-historical terms in the great work of Augustine's maturity, the *City of God* (413–26). Well before this he had divided human society into two classes, separated by their love of God or of the world (*On True Religion*, 50). In the *City of God*, he develops this division in the context of a consideration of the relation between Christianity and the empire, occasioned by the unspectacular and short-lived, but hugely significant, fall of Rome in 410 to Alaric and the Goths. Were the destinies of the church and empire providentially interwoven, and, if so, in what way? How were the pagans, who blamed the fall on Christianity, to be answered? Augustine's response looks at their historical, political, and social interaction from the perspective of divine providence and both sets Christianity apart from pagan religion (books 1–5), philosophy (6–10), and history (15–18) and demonstrates their interdependence at a social, political, and legal level (19) in virtue of the fact that fallen man is simply a pilgrim, a 'resident alien' in a fractured world, where ultimate unity, peace, and harmony cannot be attained, but only longed and hoped for. Here he must respect and use the structures that God's voluntary providence has provided—the church and its scriptures, the empire and its laws—while remembering that they are not the City of God, that the journey ends, for the elect, only in the life to come.

Works 🌿

In the intervals of the Donatist and Pelagian controversies, and in the time free from his extraordinarily onerous episcopal duties (as legal arbitrator, preacher, spiritual director, pastoral and theological adviser, and correspondent—in *Letters*, 224. 2, he tells us he devoted the day to one task and the night to another) Augustine produced the largest body of work of any writer in antiquity. A large proportion consists of sermons or works of exegesis, notably the two long series on John's gospel and the Psalms. As well as the *City of God* and the substantial body of controversial works against Manichees, Donatists, and Pelagians, he wrote hundreds of letters, made repeated attempts to interpret the first few chapters of Genesis, the high point of which is the twelve-book *Literal Commentary on Genesis* (401–14), composed fifteen books on *The Trinity* (399–419, a work which breaks startlingly new ground, and whose psychological analogies have exercised great influence in western tradition), considered the role of classical culture, literary criticism, and rhetoric in *On Christian Doctrine* (396/ 426, which was tremendously influential in the Middle Ages), wrote numerous treatises on ethical subjects, on Christian instruction, and philosophical questions. There is barely a subject that he leaves unconsidered.

Augustine died in August 430, as the Vandals, conquerors of Roman Africa, were about to occupy and devastate Hippo. His library, however, survived intact.

Western Christian thought can be seen as the history of the assimilation and rethinking of Augustine's legacy. He set the agenda for subsequent thought, and from the moment of his death his influence has been uniquely pervasive and inspiring. This is no doubt partly due to his character, the erudition, eloquence, and coherence of his work, its vast quantity and outstanding quality, his all-embracing interests, and his originality and creativity as theologian, philosopher, controversialist, mystic, and pastor. Medieval reflection on the relation of philosophy and religion, faith and reason, Reformation thought on grace and free will, works and justification, Enlightenment discussions of sin and the possibility of perfection, modern and postmodern theories of language and human motivation, as well as the perennial practice of exegesis, mysticism, and devotion: all bear the distinctive impress of his thought.

Translations can be found in *Oxford Library of the Fathers, Library of Christian Classics, Ancient Christian Writers, Fathers of the Church* series.

Augustine, *Confessions*, trans. H. Chadwick (1992).

—— *City of God*, trans. H. Bettenson (1972).

Bonner, G., *Augustine: Life and Controversies*, 2nd edn. (1986).

—— *God's Decree and Man's Destiny* (1987).

Brown, P., *Augustine of Hippo* (1967).

Burnaby, J., *Amor Dei* (1938).

Chadwick, H., *Augustine* (1986).

Clark, G., *Augustine: Confessions* (1994).

Madec, G., *Petites Études Augustiniennes* (1994).

—— *La Patrie et la Voie* (1989).

Markus, R. A., *Sacred and Secular* (1994).

—— (ed.), *Augustine: A Collection of Critical Essays* (1972).

O'Daly, G., *Augustine's Philosophy of Mind* (1987).

O'Donnell, J. J., *Confessions*, Text and Commentary vols. 1–3 (1992).

Rist, J., *Augustine: Ancient Thought Baptised* (1994).

Anselm of Canterbury

(*c*.1033–1109)

PETER CRAMER

Anselm was born in Aosta. In 1059 he found his way to the abbey of Bec in Normandy, where he was taught by Lanfranc, also an Italian. In 1063 he succeeded Lanfranc as prior, and in 1078 became abbot. Eadmer, in his *Life of Anselm*, gives a vivid account of his reluctance to take office and the care with which he none the less fulfilled his duties as a guide of souls. It was at Bec that he composed the two great theological works, the *Monologion* and the *Proslogion* (1078–9), as well as the earlier among his *Meditations* and *Prayers*, the short treatises *On the Fall of the Devil* and *On Free Will*, and the philosophical works *On Truth* and *On Grammar*. Anselm was consecrated archbishop of Canterbury in December 1093. Through his troubled tenure as archbishop, and through two periods of exile from England, he kept at his theological work, finishing *On the Incarnation of the Word* in 1095, and his third major work *Cur deus homo* (*Why God became Man*) in Italy in 1098.

His writing was always of unusual clarity and force. It has in it a curious affinity with the thought of Plato (curious because he can have known at first-hand only the *Timaeus*), has in places the form of a brilliant interpretation of Augustine's more hesitant speculations (for example on the Trinity), and evoked the interest of Kant at a time when the thinking of the Middle Ages tended to be the object of condescension.

The *Monologion* is what Anselm calls 'a meditation on the divine essence', and, in its central passages, on the Trinity. In the inward path of its meditation the mind comes upon the 'Highest Good', which it will tend naturally towards because of its own formation 'in the image of God'. Its interpretations are, as it were, tied to the 'Highest Good' or 'Highest Being', and so are in some sense bound to be true to life. The power of discerning what is true is in this way something like an emergence from the chrysalis of solipsism, of meditative introspection, into the daylight of the true being of created things and their creator.

Meditation is, however, also a reflection on words. The *Monologion* is of Anselm's writings the one that owes most to his grounding in grammar, that element in the medieval curriculum occupied with the analysis of language. In ch. 10, he asks us to recall an experience in the use of words where the mind produces an image of an existing object with such felicity that the image and its object seem to be one. Taking the thought or image as a word, a kind of speaking, Anselm understands such experiences as belonging to language at its most intense and truthful. This is 'the speaking of things' (*locutio rerum*) which appears to be making, or bringing into being, what it says. On the recollection of such moments in the use of words he now constructs his meditation. With scrutiny, the unity between word and thing is seen to be an illusion, for our words do no more than imitate what is already there. They are likenesses of things, not things themselves; like being, but not being itself. For the word which, instead of being 'after' the world, brings it into being, we have to look to the originating word of God at the moment of creation, whose quality of unity with what it creates is spelt out in the story of creation from nothing. If God makes the world from nothing, the 'word' with which he does so, since it imitates nothing that goes before it, must bring into being as it speaks. Anselm's thought here is a re-enactment of both the *Timaeus*, with its myth of creation by the demiurge, and of the opening verses of Genesis. Much of what remains of the *Monologion* is a struggle to connect this first word with the many words of our own speech which imitate it.

The guide Anselm takes on his journey is that of 'faith seeking understanding' (*fides quaerens intellectum*), a thread that runs all through his reflections. Reason here, or understanding, is not external to faith, as though a separate faculty of mind (as it might be in Abelard for example), but is implied in it, rather as sympathetic criticism is demanded of its beholder by the interrogative force of a great painting. The kinship of faith and reason has an echo in the perception by some recent philosophers (such as Gadamer, Ricœur), themselves the heirs of the 18th-century distinction between 'symbol' and 'allegory', that symbols are not dissolved by analysis but revivified. And it is a kinship borne out in the protrusion of the bible into the argument, despite Anselm's avoidance of quotation in favour of 'the necessity of reason'. The whole book might even be considered a formal reflection on the opening verses of Genesis and the seeing 'through a glass darkly' of 1 Corinthians 13: 12. With its biblical hinterland, the *Monologion* pushes to its extreme Augustine's discovery that the introspective and the biblical are not distinct. The *Monologion* is thus at bottom radical exegesis, despite its reluctance to quote the bible. Its core is a scrutiny of what it is to speak a word, and if it is exegesis it is exegesis of the bible as word.

Moreover, it is an odyssey, the story of an understanding that waxes and wanes. Towards its end, struck by what he calls 'the indigence of the name of the Trinity'—the helplessness of language before this simultaneity of three and one—Anselm concedes that we have been looking into a mirror: 'through a glass darkly.' It is the sentiment of indigence which prevails as the journey is reviewed. At the height of his odyssey, though, and with an unruffled mastery that borrows from the sublime in his subject, he turns by way of the motif of the birth of the word from its speaker (the Father), to the Trinity. Just as the speech founded in likeness is somewhere indistinguishable from that 'intimate speech' (*intima locutio*) by which God makes the world (or just as the prophet talks back, albeit stuttering, to his inspiration), so, for Anselm, the perception of the Trinity as Father giving birth to Son is not a metaphor (if metaphor is one thing *indicating* another), but a withdrawal from metaphor. Anselm proceeds by the correction of metaphor, stripping back one metaphor by the introduction of another, on the grounds that the fatherhood seen in the ascetic light of corrected metaphor is fatherhood as it is: as it is, not in its transient aspect (the fatherhoods of our biographies), but as it is in the perspective of God's art, which is uncorrupted by the passing away of what it produces. And yet this 'as it is' borrows its solidity, its warmth, its exertion of presence, from the familiar lived paternity of human biographies. The effect of these meditations on the Trinity (deepened as they are by a consideration of the Holy Spirit as the love between Father and Son) is an ascetic joy, which, for all the decline suffered in the concluding pages, is borne out in the substantiality given to the 'divine essence' by the bleakness, both linguistic and moral, felt in the 'indigence of the name of the Trinity'.

The *Proslogion* puts into the form of an argument 'a struggle of thoughts': the 'thought' of the philosophical exhaustion which settles on the mind when the object of its quest, the 'Highest Good' (or the argument which would encompass this 'Highest Good'), endlessly escapes its labours; and the 'thought' which is the mind's inevitable familiarity with God, its inability not to understand God (for it is made in the image of God, a teaching the force of which is known in the act of prayer). This 'inability not to understand' is also glimpsed in that intensest of speaking experiences hit upon already in the *Monologion*, and it is as well to read the earlier work before setting out on the later. 'In this struggle of thoughts, there offered itself what I had despaired of.' The *Proslogion* is not to be read as an argument about God or his existence. It is rather a rehearsal in the form of an argument of the discovery of God as object (though one in which the object and the process of discovery cannot be told apart). The 'one argument', as Anselm calls it to distinguish it from the less satisfactory 'chain of arguments' in the *Monologion*, is condensed in the definition (also an invocation) of God at the start of ch. 2: 'We believe you to be that thing than which nothing greater can be thought.' On this definition turns the thought, till now hidden within prayer ('When will you light up your eyes? And show us your face? When will you restore yourself to us?') that the most perfect being is also the most real. The phrase 'something than which nothing greater can be thought' is so put together, however, that it throws the mind back into struggle. The 'something' must be greater than can be thought, for otherwise it would be possible to think something greater. Yet it is this side of nothing, and therefore palpable. The mind is caught between quest, and the apprehension of God as *res*, a thing—much as Job (one might say) recovered from the misery of his incomprehension with the Lord's 'Where wast thou when I laid the foundations of the earth?' And just as Job is made to see with fierce clarity the things of the world, so too in Anselm's philosophical version there is a correspondence between God as thing and world as thing. 'Hast thou given the horse strength? . . . Canst thou make him afraid as a grasshopper? the glory of his nostrils is terrible' (Job 38: 4; 39: 19–20). The 'one argument' with which Anselm answers the fool, 'who hath said in his heart, there is no God' (Ps. 14), is perhaps best described as a recognition of what it is to pray. The *Proslogion* is thus a series of Chinese boxes: the exhaustion and revelation of the Prologue; the prayer of ch. 1, where the reality of God presses down in the texture of shame at loss and blindness ('How long wilt thou forget us, O Lord? For ever? How long wilt thou hide thy face from us?' cf. Ps. 13: 1); the objectivity of God discovered in the intellectual quest to unveil his face: 'that than which nothing greater can be thought.' In this way, it might be said that Anselm's response to the fool, who claims that 'that than which nothing greater can be thought' might only be in the mind (*in intellectu*), not in reality (*in re*) outside the mind, is ultimately to displace the fool by the saint, in whom the knowledge of perfection, taken for granted, is repeatedly made surprising, not least to himself, by miracle. The whole course of the argument recalls the delight of the painter who set out to *make* (make up), and then becomes aware that he has *found*. But there is a turn of the screw. The finding and making are put within the frame of a making from nothing (cf. *Monologion*). Perhaps the beauty of the argument is in the end in the question it poses whether the believer is himself capable of his own belief.

In *Why God became Man*, a dialogue, Anselm gives an account of why it is 'necessary' that God become man in order for man to be saved after the Fall, a proposition built up in the first place in answer to the scorn of the unbeliever at the humiliation apparently involved in God's being man and bearing the suffering of this particular man. The necessity of God's action is the mark of its dignity, Anselm maintains. It would be unbecoming if God, for example, were to rescue Adam and his kind from their predicament after Eden simply by an unconditional gesture of mercy. For this would suggest that, at least according to our intimations of what justice might really be, injustice, being subject to no law, has more freedom than justice, so that injustice is more like God, who is also not subject to law (1. 12). This line of reasoning (posing more of a problem than it solves: the problem at the centre of *Why God became Man*, how we can say of God he is acting by necessity and yet subject to no law) represents one among many styles of reasoning in the work as a whole. The work, divided into two books, has a disarming freedom, or, perhaps better, grace, which sometimes looks like digressiveness, though it never is (see the long discussion at 1. 16–18 of the restoration to their full numbers of the angels after the fall of Lucifer and his company). It is constructed on a very solid myth, a retelling of the story of reconciliation of man and God. Dismissing as implausible the old 'ransom' myth which has God tricking Satan of his dominion over man by sending his sinless son to die—Satan can have no rights over man, says Anselm, and any patching up is between man and God—Anselm gives the following version: God had to become man because the offence given in the Garden was infinite, the guilty parties finite. Only God has it in him to make it up, only man is obliged to make it up. Hence the God-man. That the offence given to God's honour (as Anselm calls it) is infinite is established with unforgiving exactness— before he ate the fruit, Adam *already* owed all he was and had, his very being, to his maker—for what he is is wholly determined by what he was made for, and that is the beatitude God had in mind for him (1. 22). Everything he might give as recompense (the fear and love which is prayer, the labour of self-denial, forgiveness of others, obedience) he owes as debts of his being at all (1. 20). Worse, what is due to God is being itself, all of being, an impossible situation indeed. 'I think we are living very dangerously,' says Boso, Anselm's interlocutor, after being led to this point. The answer—the only answer Anselm can see, though he is happy to bow to better, or 'more necessary' reasons if he hears them—is a satisfaction by one *who does not owe*, who is not under compulsion of any kind, who has in his possession the gift of being, and, owing nothing, can give it away because he *wishes* to. The infinity of God is recast as the act of will by which he gives what all being other than himself owes (1. 11).

What Anselm wants to get, he tells us, is something solid. He is the painter who paints not on water but on solid stuff (1. 4; 2. 8). And what he paints, we might say, is the solidity of Christ's willing what is necessary. The demonstration that the story must go like this, and our ability to demonstrate this without the help of what we already know of Christ—our ability, given the beginning of the story (the Fall), to complete it by careful reasoning—have convinced us that necessity informs the agony in the Garden and all the 'injuries, insults, griefs' we know to be part of the story (cf. 2. 11). The Christ of *pathos*, very characteristic of Anselm's time, is not Anselm's Christ. Grief, straitened with the precision—the coldness even—of argument, is sublime. Not sublimated: it is still there, harsh as ever, and the sublime is less of Rembrandt's *Deposition* than of Mantegna's *Entombment*.

What, though, can be made of God's acting under necessity? Here, Anselm's view depends on a distinction between necessity of cause and effect (the heavens turn, because the laws of nature turn them), and 'necessity of sequence', where one thing follows or accompanies another, because it is so (you are speaking 'necessarily', because you are speaking). God does not 'lay down his life' because he is forced to by something outside himself; rather, he acts according to a necessity which is at once a refraction of his will and a confession of what is the case. Law, justice, necessity, are not what they seem, but instead the sovereignty evident in harmony, a kind of sureness of touch—so that an eloquent, unstrained gesture gives to each protagonist of this drama (God, Adam, God-man, angels, Virgin) the insistence which is apt to each of them, robbing the drama of tension and admitting between the figures only the most profound connection. At its most profound, the connection is that of the simplicity, the facility of seeing things as they are (and as they have been and will be) and the faith which acts accordingly at a given moment in time—and of the human experience of this the Virgin, made ready to bear God by her own power to guess how the story must end, is the palpable fulfilment (2. 17–19). Perhaps no thinker has so replenished the myths which sustain belief as Anselm with his 'necessary reasons'.

Anselm, *Collected Works*, ed. F. S. Schmitt (6 vols., 1946–61).

Barth, K., *Fides Quaerens Intellectum* (1931), ET (1960).

Campbell, R., *From Belief to Understanding: A Study of Anselm's Proslogion Argument on the Existence of God* (1976).

Davies, B., and **Evans, G. R.** (eds.), *Anselm of Canterbury: The Major Works* (1998).

Eadmer, *The Life of St Anselm*, ed. R. W. Southern (1962).

Evans, G. R., *Anselm and Talking about God* (1978).

Gilbert, P., *Dire l'Ineffable: Lecture du 'Monologion' de S. Anselme* (1984).

Hopkins, J., *A Companion to the Study of St Anselm* (1972).

—— *A New Interpretative Translation of St Anselm's Monologion and Proslogion* (1986).

Luscombe, D. E., and Evans, G. R. (eds.), *Anselm, Aosta, Bec, and Canterbury* (1996).

McIntyre, J., *St Anselm and his Critics: A Re-Interpretation of the* Cur deus homo (1954).

Southern, R. W., *Saint Anselm and his Biographer: A Study of Monastic Life and Thought 1059–c.1130* (1963).

—— *Saint Anselm: A Portrait in a Landscape* (1990).

—— **and Schmitt**, F. S. (eds.), *Memorials of St Anselm* (1969).

Ward, B. (ed.), *The Prayers and Meditations of St Anselm* (1973).

VI

Thomas Aquinas (1225–1274)

BRIAN DAVIES

Aquinas is universally agreed to be one of the giants in the history of Christian thought. He has been regarded as a touchstone of Roman Catholic orthodoxy since the Council of Trent (a view of him ratified by Pope Leo XIII, in the encyclical *Aeterni Patris*, and by Vatican II). As well as being highly respected by generations of Christians of all denominations, his writings continue to be studied by thinkers with no special religious affiliation, many of whom rank him among the greatest of western philosophers.

Born in Italy, Aquinas was sent, aged 5 or 6, to study at the Benedictine abbey of Monte Cassino, where he remained until he was about 15. He then went to the University of Naples, where he encountered the full range of Aristotle's writings, which had only recently come to be studied seriously in Europe. In 1244 he joined the new Dominican Order of friars and subsequently lectured at the University of Paris from 1252 to 1259, and from 1269 to 1272. He also taught at Orvieto, Rome, and Naples, writing voluminously all the time. He died at Fossanova on 7 March 1274 *en route* to the second Council of Lyons to advise on relations between the Catholic and Orthodox churches. Ideas associated with him were condemned by ecclesiastical authorities at Paris and Oxford in 1277, but he was never formally censured. He was canonized in 1323.

As well as two long theological treatises, the *Summa Theologiae* and the *Summa contra Gentiles*, Aquinas wrote commentaries on scripture (on which he regularly lectured), a large range of short works on topics in theology and philosophy (the *Opuscula*), and several detailed studies on major theological issues (the *Quaestiones disputatae*). Using newly available translations, he wrote several commentaries on Aristotle, whose teachings he was the first Christian author to employ at length in the service of Christianity (a daring enterprise since many of his contemporaries found Aristotle's thinking inimical to it). He also produced commentaries on Proclus, Boethius, Pseudo-Dionysius, and Peter Lombard. As 20th-century scholars have come to appreciate, non-Aristotelian sources were as important an influence on Aquinas as Aristotelian ones.

Though always featuring prominently in histories of philosophy, Aquinas would not have called himself a philosopher. In his writings, 'philosophers' always fall short of the true and proper 'wisdom' to be found in the Christian revelation and the living of a life properly focused on Christ as the way to perfect happiness (*beatitudo*). But he also thought that, by using their natural ability to reason, people can arrive at important truths on which those with benefit of Christian revelation can build when talking about the final goal of human living: that they can do this, for instance, when reflecting on people and their behaviour.

On the topic of humanity in general, Aquinas relates quite especially to recent philosophy. For his views about people (including his philosophy of mind and his moral philosophy) have little in common with the tradition leading from Descartes to Hume and beyond, but much in common with the thinking of philosophers such as Wittgenstein, Ryle, and modern authors at the centre of the contemporary revival of Aristotelian ethical thinking. For Aquinas, people are not incorporeal substances distinct from their bodies. They are not ghosts in or attached to machines. They are human animals with a specific range of powers, activities, and dispositions. He believed that human beings have souls which can survive the death of their bodies, but these souls are not human individuals. 'My soul is not me', as he writes in his commentary on 1 Corinthians. He takes all living things to have souls (to be animate), for he thinks of the soul as that which is there when something is alive. Human beings are things with a special way of being alive (they have human souls), one which is not simply bodily; so people are more than bodies in motion. Yet they are essentially bodily, and to be the people they are they must be corporeal. 'For as it belongs to the very conception of "this human being" that there should be this soul, flesh and bone, so it belongs to the very conception of "human being" that there be soul, flesh, and bone' (*ST* I q. 75 a. 4). Hence, when speaking of life after death, Aquinas looks forward to the resurrection of the body.

On the question of human action, and concentrating on what we can learn by 'natural reason', Aquinas develops an Aristotelian moral philosophy focused on the notions of virtue and vice. Virtues are acquired ways of behaving (dispositions) which help us to flourish and be happy. Vices are dispositions which help us to damage ourselves and be unhappy. He is aware that vicious people might say that they are happy, and he regularly insists that those who do wrong must be doing so because they see some good for themselves in what they are doing. On his account, which is somewhat original, there is no sharp distinction to be made between intellect and will (seeing that something is the case, and acting accordingly). Our desires can determine what we see, so we are not always the best judges when it comes to what makes for our flourishing. Our views of what can make for our happiness need to be informed by an understanding of what we actually are as living human animals in a world which includes other people (he has much to say on political matters). Just as doctors will tell us that smoking or excessive drinking is not good for us, Aquinas will say that vices are not good for us. And, just as doctors will advise certain ways of behaving, Aquinas will speak favourably of virtues as things we have reasons to cultivate, reasons which stand on their own without special reference to Christian authorities.

Aquinas also thinks that we have such reasons for asserting the existence of God. He denies that knowledge of God in this life can be had on the basis of anything we might call a direct experience of God (as some of his contemporaries argued, and as some argue today). He also denies that the existence of God can be proved on the basis of an understanding of the meaning of the word 'God'—as, for example, Anselm and Bonaventure thought, and as some modern philosophers have argued. But we can demonstrate that God exists by reasoning from the world (as effect) to God (as cause).

In a famous passage (*ST* I q. 2 a. 3, often referred to as the 'five ways') he defends this thesis by drawing on largely Aristotelian arguments (though also echoing such authors as Avicenna and Maimonides) and by focusing on change, acting agents, generation and perishing, perfection and being, and the (apparently) goal-directed behaviour of non-rational things. He argues (as he does in many texts other than the *ST*) that these objects of our experience cannot be fully accounted for in ordinary mundane terms and should lead us to acknowledge a level of causality that transcends any with which we are familiar.

In the 'five ways' and elsewhere Aquinas is particularly intrigued by the fact that there is any world at all, by the fact that there is something rather than nothing. He explicitly denies that philosophy can show that the world ever began to be (cf. *De aeternitate mundi*), so does not hold that God must exist in order to have got the world going at some time in the past (though he believes that God did this). But he constantly insists that everything we can conceive of or understand is continually dependent on God for its sheer existence (*esse*). The ancient philosophers asked causal questions about things in the world, but some 'climbed higher to the prospect of being as being' and 'observed the cause of things inasmuch as they are beings, not merely as things of such a kind or quality' (*ST* I q. 44 a. 2). If something exists, Aquinas argues, its existence either follows from its nature or is brought about by something other than itself. Aquinas then maintains that there cannot be an endless series of things bringing about the existence of others while themselves being brought about by something else. There has to be something which exists by nature. Following the biblical tradition, he calls this 'God'. In doing so, he was the first Christian author seriously, and in detail, to focus on the notion of existence as of primary importance for reflecting on God, whom he speaks of as 'Being Itself' (*ipsum esse subsistens*).

Among other things, this strand in Aquinas's thinking leads him to insist that free human actions are caused by God. He frequently alludes to arguments suggesting that people cannot be free under God's providence (cf. *De malo*, 6). He replies to such arguments by affirming that the reality of providence (i.e. the reality of God working in all things as first cause and sustainer) is not incompatible with human freedom. People have freedom (a conclusion for which he argues at length); yet God really does act in everything. And since 'everything' includes human free actions, God works in them as much as in anything else.

People are in charge of their acts, including those of willing and of not willing, because of the deliberative activity of reason, which can be turned to one side or the other. But that someone should deliberate or not deliberate, supposing that one were in charge of this too, would have to come about by a preceding deliberation. And since this may not proceed to infinity, one would finally have to reach the point at which a person's free decision is moved by some external principle superior to the human mind, namely by God, as Aristotle himself demonstrated. Thus the minds even of healthy people are not so much in charge of their acts as not to need to be moved by God.   (*ST* I–II q. 109 a. 3)

God 'causes everything's activity inasmuch as he gives it the power to act, maintains it in existence, applies it to its activity, and inasmuch as it is by his power that every other power acts' (*De potentia*, 3. 7). This teaching is not incompatible with belief in human freedom. What is incompatible with that is 'necessity of coercion', the effect of violence, as when something acts on one and 'applies force to the point where one cannot act otherwise' (*ST* I q. 82 a. 1). Freely acting human persons are not under the influence of some other *creature*. They are made to be what they are by God, who is responsible both for freely acting agents and for things which act of necessity. God's will 'is to be thought of as existing outside the realm of existents, as a cause from which pours forth everything that exists in all its variant forms' (*Commentary on Aristotle's* De interpretatione, I 14). Freely acting people are one among many forms of existent. They are free *because of* God, not *in spite of* him.

Aquinas is somewhat reserved in his account of what we can know of God by human reason. 'The knowledge that is natural to us has its source in the senses and extends just so far as it can be led by sensible things; from these, however, our understanding cannot reach to the divine essence' (*ST* I q. 12 a. 12). God 'is greater than all we can say, greater than all we can know; and not merely does he transcend our language and our knowledge, but he is beyond the comprehension of every mind whatsoever, even of angelic minds, and beyond the being of every substance' (*Commentary on Dionysius'* Divine Names, 1. 3. 77). But Aquinas also offers a range of philosophical arguments for the truth of a number of affirmative statements about God. He holds, for example, that God can be proved to be perfect, good, one, living, omnipotent, loving, changeless, eternal, omniscient, and free. Though we cannot know God's essence in this life we can speak of God by using certain words which we normally use when talking of creatures since there is positive reason for doing so and since some words can apply literally to creatures and to God by analogy, i.e. without signifying exactly the same reality, but without signifying something completely different either (cf. *ST* I q. 13).

But 'man's ultimate happiness does not consist in that knowledge of God whereby he is known by all or many in a vague kind of opinion, nor again in that knowledge whereby he is known in the speculative sciences through demonstration' (*Summa contra Gentiles*, 3. 48). So having explained that God can be known to exist by reason, Aquinas attempts to say how it can be thought that God is Father, Son, and Holy Spirit. Then he turns to the Incarnation. For him, the doctrines of the Trinity and the Incarnation cannot be demonstrated to be true (he argues that they are demonstrably indemonstrable). But he takes them to be true, and much of his work is an attempt to expound them, to defend them from charges of inconsistency and comparable criticisms, and to indicate their implications.

Aquinas's teaching on the Trinity is partly an attempt to say how God can be three 'persons', though 'God' is not the name of a class of which there can be more than one member. Drawing on what he thinks can be known of God by reason, and echoing such writers as Augustine, Boethius, and Anselm, he defends the claim that the persons of the Trinity are distinct 'subsisting relations'. Primarily, however (and with much reference to biblical and patristic texts), Aquinas sees the Trinity as a life of knowledge and love which shares itself with creatures and does so in a special way with people. Absolutely distinct from creatures, the Trinity needs nothing for its perfection. But through the grace of God people can be brought to share in what it is. There is 'a special love by which God draws the rational creature above its natural condition to have a part in the divine goodness . . . By this love God, simply speaking, wills for the creature that eternal good which is himself' (*ST* I–II q. 110 a. 1). Aquinas develops a detailed account of how Christ is the embodiment of God's will in this respect.

Again drawing on truths about God which he takes to be knowable by reason, and with much logical dexterity, he defends the claim that

Christ is one divine subject with two natures (cf. *ST* III q. 16). Then he develops an account of Christ as teacher and example to be followed. With an eye on the biblical teaching that 'Christ died for our sins', he also writes at length on the notion of Christ as saviour. Very conscious of human evil and divine goodness, Aquinas is clear that sin is a barrier between people and God. Unlike many theologians, however, he denies that the obstacle could only be removed by the death of Christ. 'Simply and absolutely speaking, God could have freed us otherwise than by Christ's passion, for nothing is impossible with God' (*ST* III q. 46 a. 2).

Aquinas argues that Christ's death deals with sin because it was the death of God incarnate and thus God's expression of his eternal love for sinners. Rare among medieval authors, he maintains that human redemption is achieved simply by the fact of the Incarnation, though (1) he finds sense in claims that the death of Christ 'satisfies' for the sin of human beings (a notion very prominent in the work of Anselm), and (2) he makes much of the concepts 'priest', 'sacrifice', and 'redeemer' when speaking of Christ's work. His basic position is that Christ, being God, is God drawing people to himself (which is what he means by 'grace'), and therefore saving them simply by existing. Christ's human nature is 'an instrument of the Godhead, even as the body is the instrument of the soul' (*Summa contra Gentiles*, 4. 41). It saves simply by being there, and as long as people conform themselves to what it is and act accordingly. He also stresses that, as well as being a direct cause of grace, Christ is head of the church. At the centre of his ecclesiology, which is fundamentally a christology, this thought is developed with a focus on the notion that the merit and grace of Christ is the merit and grace of those who believe in him (cf. *ST* III q. 19 a. 4). Frequently alluding to 2 Peter 1: 4, and resembling Greek rather than western theologians, Aquinas is fond of stressing that the full effect of the Incarnation is the 'deification' of people (cf. *ST* I–II q. 112 a. 1). With this thought in mind, he develops his theories on human virtues noted above to explain how they are crowned by the 'theological virtues' of faith, hope, and charity.

Virtues are dispositions (*habitus*) for living well, and theological virtues are no exception. But, unlike the virtues of which he speaks with acknowledgement to Aristotle, they cannot be acquired and preserved by natural human effort (cf. *ST* I–II q. 112). They are wholly the work of God: they are 'infused'. We have them because grace has been given to us. And they equip us, not for the natural bodily life of rational animals, but for a sharing in the life of God. Although God could have united himself with human beings in a different way, this sharing in God's life is an effect of the life, death, and Resurrection of Christ and the sending of the Holy Spirit (the establishing of the 'New Law'). Its special mark is the presence of charity, conceived as a friendship (*amicitia*) with God and a living out of the love which God essentially is as Father, Son, and Spirit (cf. *ST* II–II q. 24 a. 2). Copiously drawing on Aristotle and other ancient philosophers, and with highly sophisticated discussions of topics such as choice, will, emotion, and intention, Aquinas dwells on this thought to offer (especially in *ST* I–II and II–II, which some regard as his greatest achievement) an account of human perfection which reflects what he finds in scripture and patristic sources and which is remarkable for its hugely intelligent weaving together of philosophical and theological ideas and arguments.

Aquinas was one of the greatest thinkers ever produced by the Christian church. His literary achievement was immense, and his impact as a Christian theologian is second only to Augustine's. Yet, in spite of his intellectual strengths, he was clearly opposed to the notion that the powers of human reason are of ultimate significance. He describes the *ST* as a textbook for beginners who need an uncluttered overview of basic Christian truths. He constantly insists that it is our love of God, not our knowledge of him, which matters in this life, which may account for the fact that he was a profound influence on such writers as John of the Cross and Meister Eckhart. He was probably the author of the Roman liturgical Office of Corpus Christi (revised in the 15th century), and possibly the author of the popular hymn 'Adoro te devote'. More people are familiar with these last two works, or at least parts of them, than with his writings as introduced above. This is, perhaps, to use a favourite word of his, fitting (*conveniens*).

Aquinas, Thomas, *Opera Omnia*, Leonine edn. (Rome, 1882–).

—— *Summa Theologiae*, Blackfriars edn. Latin and English with notes and introductions (61 vols., 1964–80).

Bourke, Vernon J., *Thomistic Bibliography: 1920–1940*, The Modern Schoolman (1921).

Chenu, M.-D., *Towards Understanding Saint Thomas*, ET (1964).

Congar, Yves, *Thomas d'Aquin: Sa vision de théologie et de l'Église* (1984).

Davies, Brian, *The Thought of Thomas Aquinas* (1992).

Elders, Leo J., *The Philosophical Theology of St. Thomas Aquinas* (1990).

Gilson, Étienne, *The Christian Philosophy of St Thomas Aquinas* (1957).

Ingardia, Richard (ed.), *Thomas Aquinas: International Bibliography 1977–1990* (1993).

Kretzmann, Norman, and Stump, Eleonore (eds.), *The Cambridge Companion to Aquinas* (1993).

Mandonnet, P., and Destrez, J., *Bibliographie Thomiste*, 2nd edn., rev. M.-D. Chenu (1960).

Miethe, Terry L., and Bourke, Vernon J., *Thomistic Bibliography, 1940–1978* (1980).

McDermott, Timothy (ed.), *Aquinas: Selected Philosophical Writings* (1993).

Torrell, Jean-Pierre, *Saint Thomas Aquinas i. The Person and His Work*, ET (1996).

—— *Saint Thomas d'Aquin: Maître spirituel* (1996).

Weisheipl, James A., *Friar Thomas D'Aquino* (1974); republished with Corrigenda and Addenda (1983).

VII

Martin Luther (c.1483–1546)

EUAN CAMERON

A theologian and preacher, Martin Luther inaugurated the Reformation of the 16th century, and was the founding figure of the Lutheran churches.

Luther to c.1520

Martin Luther was born in Eisleben in the county of Mansfeld, to a family involved in leasing the copper-mining businesses of the region. He was schooled in Mansfeld, Magdeburg, and Eisenach, and in 1501 entered the University of Erfurt. In summer 1505, after some sort of mental crisis and contrary to his family's wishes, Luther abruptly entered the house of reformed Augustinian Eremites at Erfurt. Ordained priest in 1507, he began to study theology, and quickly acquired the minor degrees in the discipline. In 1510/11 he made a brief visit to Rome on his order's business. Soon afterwards he transferred permanently to the monastery and university at Wittenberg in Saxony, where he had already taught briefly, and took his doctorate in theology there.

53

Thereafter he served as a professor of theology and preacher in Wittenberg for the rest of his life.

Luther began to deliver twice-weekly lectures from winter 1513/14 onwards. Notes from his lectures on *Psalms* (1513–15), *Romans* (1515–16), *Galatians* (1516–17), *Hebrews* (1517–18), and a further series on *Psalms* (?1518/19–21) survive, though these cannot all be dated with absolute precision, and some other lectures may have been lost. Through Luther's lectures, scholars have shown how he gradually emancipated himself from the theology of his training, then shaped a challenge to late medieval Catholicism. Luther was educated in the *via moderna*, derived from the 14th-century Oxford theologian William of Ockham. Many in this tradition resolved the paradox of divine grace and human response in justification by reasoning that God's grace lay in his promise to reward, especially through the sacraments, people's inadequate but 'semi-meritorious' efforts to love God. By its stress on the initial effort of the pious soul, this school encouraged the voluntary acts of devotion popular in the contemporary church.

Luther grew progressively more dissatisfied with this view, perhaps influenced by some within his Augustinian Order who argued for the spontaneous work of divine grace within the believer. By 1515–16 he taught that God's indwelling grace 'healed' the soul, in a manner reminiscent of Augustine's anti-Pelagian tracts. In 1516–18 he attacked the 'scholastic' theology of his early training. By 1518–19 his thought had moved further, reaching its mature form by 1520–1.

In conversations later in life, and in his 1545 autobiographical sketch, Luther described a sudden flash of insight, in which he had realized that 'God's righteousness . . . revealed [in the Gospel]' (Rom. 1: 17) meant not God's terrifying righteous condemnation of sin, but the divine gift of innocence or acquittal, offered through faith. This flash of insight, sometimes called the 'tower-experience' (*Turmerlebnis*) cannot be dated securely on the basis of the contemporary lectures or correspondence. Luther appears, with hindsight, to have invented a spiritualized oversimplification of his prolonged spiritual development.

While Luther was developing his personal theological perspective, a relatively peripheral issue forced him into public view. In autumn 1517 sales of the great indulgence to support the rebuilding of St Peter's basilica in Rome were renewed in the territory of the archbishop-elector of Mainz, partly to help the newly elevated Archbishop Albrecht of Brandenburg recover the costs of his installation. Papal indulgences exempted living people, on payment of an individually assessed fee, from penances imposed at previous confessions. However, since around 1480 indulgences had been extended to departed souls presumed to be in purgatory, in the belief that they might also shorten or terminate penances in the hereafter. Mainz territory included Erfurt, adjoining Saxony, and Luther was asked to give an opinion on the claims of the indulgence preachers.

On 31 October 1517 Luther wrote to the archbishop a respectful request that he restrain and correct his preachers' over-enthusiasm, and enclosed ninety-five 'theses' (short academic propositions) for disputation on the power of indulgences. It is not certain that the theses were also, as tradition claims, fixed to the door of the Wittenberg castle-church and formally disputed. Luther did send them privately to his friends, and soon single-leaf printed versions appeared in at least four cities. However pugnaciously phrased, the ninety-five theses were technical propositions in school Latin, not a populist manifesto. They stirred up a storm because the Dominican Order saw Luther's criticism of its indulgence-preachers as a slight, and immediately sought his condemnation at Rome as a heretic.

The papacy responded with heavy-handed authoritarianism combined with diplomatic appeasement of Luther's prince, the elector of Saxony, and a failure seriously to address the theological issues. Luther, called on simply to recant by the papal legate Cajetan in October 1518, without being given convincing reasons, instead questioned the basis for the pope's authority. Accused by the Ingolstadt theologian Johann Eck at the Leipzig disputation (June 1519) of repeating the heresy of the Bohemian John Huss, Luther also lost confidence in church councils like the one where Huss had been condemned. Pope Leo X provisionally excommunicated Luther on 15 June 1520. Summoned to the German *Reichstag* at Worms in April 1521, Luther refused to withdraw his writings, unless shown to be in error according to 'Scripture or evident reason'.

Though soon afterwards condemned by the church and outlawed by the emperor, Luther's reputation prospered in Germany because of the discredit and ridicule in which many of his opponents were held, especially by advanced intellectuals influenced by the northern Renaissance. His accessible style in Latin and German won him a readership even among those who had not grasped the core of his ideas, nor foreseen their destructive impact on traditional religion.

Luther and the Reformation challenge *c.*1520–1 🖋

Before appearing at Worms, Luther issued pamphlets and manifestos that won him support, at least partly because he appeared to echo calls for change already widely expressed. In *To the Christian Nobility of the German Nation*, written in the summer of 1520, Luther cut the knot which had prevented the political leaders of German society from redressing faults in the church, despite repeated protests made by the *Reichstag* to Rome since the 1450s. The clergy, he argued, had claimed that they, the ordained, sacrosanct priesthood, were the church: that they alone could govern, discipline, or reform themselves. Yet this claim was 'deceit and hypocrisy'. All Christians were equally 'spiritual', though differing in their functions. Consequently, a priest was merely a representative of the shared 'priesthood' inherent in the whole community. Luther then concluded that the community should go ahead and reshape its religious life without reference to pope or hierarchy.

Secondly, Luther's programme appealed to Renaissance intellectuals who had learned, especially under the influence of Erasmus, to be sceptical of the materialism of popular piety, and to despise contemporary theology. Luther's attack on indulgences reached readers who already doubted whether time to be spent in purgatory could be calculated precisely. He proposed that the local shrines of Germany, such as those of the bleeding eucharistic hosts at Wilsnack or the miraculous image of the Virgin at Regensburg, should be demolished; many intellectuals already mocked bogus miracles. Above all, Luther's campaign to reform academic theology, by replacing medieval scholastic systematizers with the early fathers and literary exposition of the bible, struck a chord with contemporary Christian humanism.

However, the resemblances with anticlerical, nationalistic, or humanist programmes were superficial. Luther's critique of contemporary sacerdotalism rested on a fundamentally new definition of the 'righteousness' that saved the soul. This definition was expressed in its mature form (in the opinion of most recent scholars) in the sermon 'On twofold righteousness' of 1519, lyrically and accessibly in *On Christian Freedom*, written in October 1520, and with greatest technical precision in *Against Latomus*, written in 1521 during his protective custody after the Worms *Reichstag*. A very influential statement of Luther's view appeared in the first edition of the *Common Places* published by Luther's younger Wittenberg colleague Philip Melanchthon, also in 1521.

Whereas recent theology usually viewed justification in terms of inner purification through grace and sacrament, Luther defined justification as the merciful forgiveness of God given to those who were really still sinners. Righteousness was a 'cloak', something extrinsic or 'alien' to the soul, draped over its continuing sinfulness, and apprehended through faith. One who trusted in this forgiveness was free from the obligation to perform 'works' that tried to 'earn' salvation. However, those who were saved would naturally overflow in acts of love towards

God and their neighbour, even though this 'sanctification' was incomplete and inadequate. The sacraments (reduced from the traditional seven to two, baptism and the Eucharist, by Luther's *On the Babylonian Captivity of the Church* of 1520) offered tangible seals and pledges of justification.

These teachings wielded astonishing power to destroy old modes of thought and alter the priorities of the religious life. Late medieval western Catholicism leaned heavily on the objective value of pious works—sacramental penance, masses for the soul, the veneration of saints, and the cult of relics and other 'holy things'. Luther's teaching exploded this whole edifice. In its place he stressed the reading and exposition of scripture, to learn, understand, and trust the promises of the gospel. Scripture, he argued, was authoritative of itself and by itself, because of the message of Christ contained in it. No tradition of approved Catholic exegesis, or extra-scriptural revelation, was admitted. Luther's German translation of the bible, issued in parts from 1522, was by no means the first vernacular version, but soon superseded earlier translations wherever his message was received. He urged communal worship, private prayer, and neighbourly charity. Private masses were soon abolished; worship took place in the vernacular, though Luther made this change deliberately slowly.

The abandonment of the Catholic principle, that divine power is mediated through a reliable church, abolished sacral priesthood. It justified assimilating clerics into lay society, something eagerly embraced by city and princely governments alike. The estate of the clergy turned into the qualified profession of married, often middle-class, and endogamous parish pastors. The hierarchy was drastically simplified; monastic orders were abolished. The visible church became coterminous with the lay political community, whether a city-state, principality, or kingdom. Lay authorities took responsibility for social tasks formerly the church's preserve, such as education and the relief of the poor. Luther did not have a high view of the state's role in religious matters. In his *On Secular Authority* of 1523, he regarded the realm of the spiritual Christian as quite separate from political life: faith could not be coerced, and secular powers could not legislate in the spiritual sphere. Nevertheless, his rejection of political power for the 'clergy' led inescapably to lay management of the visible church.

These changes did not take place at once, though many communities, especially German city-states, took some decisive steps in these directions by the mid-1520s. The ideal of the self-governing lay community assuming spiritual responsibility for its priesthood was appropriated by some articulate leaders of the peasant uprisings which began in Swabia in autumn 1524 and flared up across Germany in the spring of 1525. The literate adaptation of this ideal for the peasants' programme owed something to the reformers of southern Germany and Switzerland, more influenced by Zwingli than Luther. Luther observed the peasant revolt in the violent millenarian form which it assumed in nearby Thuringia. Quite literally believing the devil to be at work there, he urged secular rulers to use extreme force against recalcitrant rebels. After the brutal suppression of the revolts in 1525–6, while popular reformation movements continued, especially in the cities, the tone changed subtly. Fewer lay people published spontaneously on religious themes; recognized authority tightened its grasp on the movement.

The definition and characteristics of Lutheranism 🌿

In the later 1520s Luther's task changed. Rather than produce new insights of shattering importance, he had to define his position precisely; to contradict 'false brethren' among the reformers whose teachings threatened to outflank and supersede his own; and to respond to the untidy exigencies of the political context. In none of these contexts was he at ease. As a group of cities and princes coalesced in 1529–30 as the core of the 'Lutheran' states, a foundation document was produced, the *Confession of Augsburg* submitted to the emperor and the *Reichstag* in 1530. This conciliatory document was drawn up not by Luther (though he approved it) but by Philip Melanchthon. The *Instructions to the Visitors* of 1528, which laid much of the groundwork for the Saxon church, were also Melanchthon's work. Melanchthon was more confident than Luther in the work of church-building, and more ready to accept princes as fellow-workers in reform. Another associate, Johann Bugenhagen, performed similar work for the churches of north Germany and Scandinavia. However, as the visitations of 1528 revealed the appalling ignorance of priests and people, Luther wrote in 1529 two *Catechisms*, a short version for rote learning and a long one to inform preachers, both definitive for the Lutheran tradition.

Luther gave the 'Lutheran' churches a distinctive character through controversy. The debate provoked by Erasmus's *On Free Will* of 1525 had little historical significance: most humanists had already taken a stance *vis-à-vis* Luther's message. The controversy with Oecolampadius and Zwingli over the sacraments, especially the Eucharist, in 1527–9 was momentous. Luther's response to those who denied a physical, bodily presence of Christ in the Eucharist was fatefully determined by his earliest confrontation on this subject with an estranged colleague, Andreas Karlstadt. Thereafter he could not respect anyone whose views resembled Karlstadt's. Luther needed to believe in a physical, objective presence of Christ as the guarantee of justification. He regarded rational argument that expounded away the words 'this is my body' as an arrogant misuse of 'harlot' reason. Philip of Hesse's effort to bring Luther to agree a common position with Zwingli and the Swiss at the Colloquy of Marburg in 1529 failed on this issue, alone of all the topics discussed. Followers of Luther, especially Johannes Brenz, would develop the doctrine of the 'ubiquity' of Christ's risen body, and the insistence that even the unworthy truly ate the body, and keep the Lutheran and Calvinist traditions at a hostile distance well into the next century.

Luther bequeathed to the Lutheran churches a style of worship that distinguished them from the south Germans and Swiss. He was a liturgical conservative in communal worship: he insisted on teaching the people before introducing changes. His German mass-order (1525–6) stripped out any suggestion of propitiatory sacrifice, but left such traditional elements as were not clearly offensive. He objected to the ritual destruction of images and legalistic objection to pictures, found in the Swiss reformations. Lutheran churches retained much of their medieval ornamentation; Lutheran religious books used illustrations quite freely. Luther made a vital contribution to the musical heritage of the Protestant churches. In contrast to Calvinism, where scriptural texts and above all the psalms formed the core of sung worship, Luther readily wrote new hymns of his own and encouraged others to do so. By the late 1520s Luther had written some two dozen hymns, including the famous *Ein feste Burg*. The richness of later German church music may safely be traced to his influence.

Luther's personal qualities

In certain respects Luther's personal preferences and attitudes were not normative for the Lutheran churches, and posed problems in his own lifetime and after. Recent scholarship has shown how Luther viewed the world as the theatre of a cosmic struggle between divine and demonic spirits. In controversy he opposed not just his adversary, but the 'spirit', the 'devil', which he saw behind the adversary. He saw 'diabolical' assaults from within his own camp as proof that the true gospel was being preached. This led him to assimilate his opponents to each other, and not to take their subtleties seriously.

Luther may also have regarded this cosmic struggle of the gospel and the devil as a sign of the imminent end of the world (especially in 1520, 1531, and c.1540). In this context, Luther saw his role as being to preach the gospel in the face of the devil's assaults, until Christ appeared as the true 'reformer'. If this view of Luther is correct, his apocalyptic outlook does account for Luther's relative indifference to outward forms, and his sublime lack of concern for the political security of the Reformation.

Luther's spirituality could be highly subjective. Having arrived at his understanding of the gospel through an immense inner struggle, he had no respect for others whose consciences were not similarly 'captive to the Word of God', if this meant that they could play with the meaning of scripture in their sacramental theology. He regarded the 'true Christians' in this world as a minority, lost among the majority of the indifferent. Yet the reluctance of so many either to heed his preaching, or to show any improvement in their lives after hearing him, also caused him fits of depression (for instance in 1527) and prompted him to abandon preaching entirely for a time (in 1529–30).

Concern at the limited impact of the gospel may also help to explain his abusive writings against the Jews, which reached a peak in 1543. These seem to have been motivated by a fear that Jewish exegetes of the OT might shake the faith of Christians. Luther's hostility, however, focused on the religious teaching of Judaism, not the mythical child-murders which were the stuff of contemporary anti-Jewish fantasy. Luther used increasingly foul and abusive language in many of his later polemics, whatever the target, apparently as a calculated and deliberate tactic.

Assessment 🌿

Luther died in 1546, just before the Emperor Charles V won a military victory over the Lutheran League of Schmalkalden. Military defeat, and the ambiguity of Luther's legacy, provoked a thirty-year split in the Lutheran churches between moderate revisionists led initially by Melanchthon, and a hardline faction that exaggerated many of Luther's personal idiosyncrasies. Up to the Reformation centenary celebrations of 1617 and beyond, he became more and more of an icon, a miraculous figure revered and canonized by his followers.

Luther's core insight, in various ways rediscovered or reinvented in all the Protestant traditions, decisively shifted the paradigm of Christian thought in northern Europe away from the Catholic concept of divine grace transmitted through Holy Church, and changed the whole religious culture built on that concept. The insight, and its expression through exegesis and preaching, mark Luther as a theologian of genius. Without his tenacity and conviction, this insight, 'the Word' as he saw it, might not have achieved its effect. Yet the converse side to Luther's nature, his apocalyptic vision, his almost Manichaean attitude to opponents, left his church with a difficult inheritance. His heirs, in Lutheran and Reformed traditions alike, have often found it expedient to use his legacy selectively.

Althaus, P., *The Theology of Martin Luther*, ET (1966).

Brecht, Martin, *Martin Luther: His Road to Reformation, 1483–1521* (1981), ET (1985).

—— *Martin Luther: Shaping and Defining the Reformation, 1521–1532* (1986), ET (1990).

—— *Martin Luther: The Preservation of the Church, 1532–1546* (1987), ET (1993).

Cargill Thompson, W. J. D., *The Political Thought of Martin Luther*, ed. P. Broadhead (1984).

Edwards, Mark U., *Luther and the False Brethren* (1975).

—— *Luther's Last Battles: Politics and Polemics, 1531–46* (1983).

Harran, Marilyn J., *Luther on Conversion: The Early Years* (1983).

Hendrix, Scott H., *Luther and the Papacy: Stages in a Reformation Conflict* (1981).

Oberman, Heiko A., *Luther: Man between God and the Devil* (1982), ET (1989).

—— *The Reformation: Roots and Ramifications* (1986), ET (1994).

Steinmetz, D. C., *Luther and Staupitz: An Essay in the Intellectual Origins of the Protestant Reformation* (1980).

Huldrych Zwingli (1484–1531)

ALFRED SCHINDLER

The Protestant Reformer, Zwingli, was born in the Toggenburg valley, Lower Alps, now in the Swiss canton of St Gallen. His family belonged to the upper ranks of the peasantry, and Toggenburg had numerous links with the Swiss confederacy. This background explains why Zwingli, throughout his life, felt he had a right and duty to engage in politics, and why he saw Switzerland as his fatherland. Maintaining his country's independence and restoring it to true godliness were supreme goals of his life.

Zwingli studied at Bern, Vienna, and Basel; after a brief period of theological study he was ordained priest and worked from 1506 at Glarus, from 1516 at Maria Einsiedeln. He was influenced by scholasticism, especially that of Duns Scotus, and subsequently by humanism, later above all by Erasmus, whom he knew personally.

On 1 January 1519 he was appointed people's priest at the Great Minster in Zürich. His battle against the supplying of Swiss mercenaries, especially the contract with France, involved him in Zürich's politics. All his life he fought against this 'commerce', which, while highly profitable to the upper classes, sent many young men, perhaps to a life of adventure, but often to death or permanent injury.

He was fully aware of the Reformation starting in 1517 in Luther's circle, but Luther's theology had limited influence on him. Various reformist innovations (such as breach of the fasting laws) were introduced in Zürich in 1522, and in 1523 the Reformation arrived in the shape of two great Disputations—the first example ever of a successful 'city reformation'. Zwingli had been a decisive influence throughout.

It soon became clear that the people later called Anabaptists, while in basic agreement with Zwingli, were prepared to surrender the bond between civic society and the Christian community, a choice that Zwingli would not endorse. While a catholic front was gaining strength in the Swiss Confederation, there was now another opposition in Zürich itself. Doctrinal differences with Luther, particularly over the Eucharist, became increasingly obvious through their writings. The Colloquy of Marburg (1529) failed to resolve these differences, which severely hampered the formation of a Protestant alliance. Zwingli's entanglement in confessional alliance politics and in the drift towards war in Switzerland resulted in his death at the Battle of Kappel, 11 October 1531.

For the final establishment of the Reformation, Zürich must thank Zwingli's successor, Heinrich Bullinger (1504–75). The *Consensus Tigurinus* between him and Calvin (1549) led to Reformed Protestantism's bearing the stamp of Calvinism rather than 'Zwinglianism', despite Bullinger's international reputation.

The starting-point for Zwingli's theology and personal piety is God's sovereignty. Nothing can hinder God's foreknowledge and election. His activity embraces even negative factors in history and extends beyond the church. The working of his Holy Spirit can be recognized in the pagan philosophers and heroes; it is not confined within sacramental actions. This is not in any way to question the unique salvific work of Jesus Christ accomplished in his Incarnation, vicarious death,

Resurrection, and bodily presence in heaven. The dogma of the Trinity, Father, Son, and Spirit, and the two natures, unconfused and undivided, of the Redeemer are accepted as in the early centuries. Zwingli believed that at that time the principle of scriptural authority, *sola scriptura*, was still in control.

This concept of God excludes any divinization of creatures such as the Roman Catholic veneration of the saints, sacramentalism, and hierarchy. For Zwingli, Luther's clinging to the real presence of Christ's body and blood in the supper is 'papistical'. The working of the Spirit in Christians is independent of any rite; it is God's free act, owing nothing to human merit.

Equally fundamental with God's sovereignty is God's covenant with humanity. The people of God in the OT and NT is one single covenant people; infant baptism corresponds to circumcision. Hence the Anabaptists are wrong to attach conditions to it. Their separating themselves from the people as a whole is also to be rejected. The word of God, as recovered in the Reformation, is urgently necessary for the well-being of the *res publica*, in Zürich and throughout Switzerland.

Nevertheless, Zwingli is not for theocracy in the proper sense nor for holy war. Divine and human justice must be clearly distinguished. That which is, without qualification, good in God's sight—in the sense of the Sermon on the Mount—and our justification by grace alone are sharply differentiated from political action. Compensatory adjustments to society (care for the poor, including distribution of monastic wealth) and education at school and university level are indispensable for a healthy community life, as is control of morals, but not, as in Calvin's model, as part of church discipline. Zwingli was not a puritan.

Some features of Zwingli's teaching that did not pass over into Calvinist orthodoxy are: stress on election rather than rejection in the doctrine of predestination; restriction of the effect of original sin to the corruption of nature, with guilt attaching only to actual sins; the possible salvation of pious pagans.

His death in battle immediately prompted hostile polemic from his opponents, and glorification and talk of martyrdom by his supporters. Both are unjustified. His death was more in the nature of an accident. He saw himself as a prophet, meaning one who interprets God's word. This makes him neither 'political' nor 'apolitical' in the modern sense. From the Enlightenment onwards, his type of 'rational' Reformation gained in appeal. Particularly as regards eucharistic theology, a large proportion of modern Protestants are in fact Zwinglians.

Zwingli, H., *Writings*, ET, i. *The Defence of the Reformed Faith*; ii. *In Search of True Religion: Reformation, Pastoral and Eucharistic Writings* (1984).

Gäbler, U., *Huldrych Zwingli: His Life and Work*, ET (1987).

Stephens, W. P., *The Theology of Huldrych Zwingli* (1986).

—— *Zwingli: An Introduction to his Thought* (1992).

IX

John Calvin (1509–1564)

B. A. GERRISH

The Reformer of Geneva and one of the foremost theologians of the Reformation era, Calvin became the leading spokesman of the Reformed, as distinct from the Lutheran, churches. His influence on the course of the Protestant Reformation reached far beyond Geneva through his correspondence and disciples. His achievements as a biblical commentator and theologian have given some of his writings the status of enduring classics of Christian literature.

French by birth, Calvin was sent to Paris for his education and was expected to enter the service of the church. But his father's plans for him changed, and he moved to Orléans and Bourges to study law. When the father died (1531), Calvin returned to Paris and embarked on the literary career of a classical scholar, publishing his first book in 1532, a commentary on Seneca's *De clementia* ('On Clemency'). Two years later he wrote his first statement of evangelical faith, an elegant preface to the French translation of the New Testament by his cousin Pierre Robert (Olivetari). Sometime between 1532 (probably) and 1534 he had undergone the 'sudden conversion' of which he wrote in the autobiographical preface to his *Commentary on the Psalms* (1557). He continued to see himself as a writer, though now in the cause of 'pure religion', and in the summer of 1535, at the age of 26, he handed the first edition of his *Institutes* to a printer in Basel. But the following year a detour on a journey from Paris to Strasbourg took him to Geneva and changed the course of his life, forcing the reserved scholar to become a man of action. Hearing of his presence in the city, William Farel enlisted his services in the cause of the Genevan reformation with the warning that God would curse his quiet, scholarly life if he refused. Save for a brief interruption when Farel and Calvin were both dismissed by the civil authorities, Calvin devoted the rest of his years to the reform of Geneva.

Calvin's literary productivity was by no means impeded by his labours as a reformer. He was far from being a man of a single book, but his reputation rests largely on the work familiarly known as his *Institutes*. (The Latin title, *Institutio Christianae religionis*, properly means '*Instruction* in the Christian Religion'.) The first edition (1536) might be described as a manual for enquirers, but the time of its appearance, during persecution of the French Protestants, lent it also the character of an apology. A modest volume of six chapters, it was evidently modelled on Martin Luther's catechisms (1529). Luther had added to the traditional expositions of the Ten Commandments, the Creed, and the Lord's Prayer two chapters on the sacraments. Calvin departed from him in treating the two evangelical sacraments together and devoting a separate section to the five spurious 'Roman' sacraments. He then concluded with a remarkable chapter, very much his own, on Christian freedom in relation to ecclesiastical power and the civil government. Preoccupation with the sacraments and church order was to remain a distinctive mark of Calvin's theology, and the prefatory address to the French king, Francis, attests another characteristic: the ease with which Calvin could marshal the opinions of the early Christian fathers in support of the Reformation cause.

The second main edition of the *Institutes*, published while Calvin was living in Strasbourg (1539), was greatly enlarged and had a different readership in mind. In seventeen chapters Calvin offered interpretations of key biblical concepts (providence, faith, Christian freedom, and so on) to help theological students find their way in the scriptures. His model now was the *Loci communes* (theological 'commonplaces') of Luther's associate, Philip Melanchthon, first published in 1521.

The definitive edition of the *Institutes* (1559) adopts a quite different arrangement, in eighty chapters. The correlative knowledge of God and knowledge of ourselves, in which nearly all our wisdom consists, is ordered by the distinction between knowing God as creator and knowing God as redeemer. Knowledge of the creator is the theme of book 1. Books 2–4 deal with God the redeemer from three perspectives: redemption through Christ, faith in Christ, and the means of grace. The order intended, however, is not the actual order of knowing. Calvin held that a sound knowledge of God the creator is possible only for believers, redeemed by Christ. An experiential sequence, then, would need to begin with book 4 and end with book 1—reading the *Institutes* backwards, so to say. It was partly the weight of tradition that led Calvin to follow the order he did, and it has often been pointed out that the sequence of the four books corresponds roughly to the order of the Apostles' Creed.

Attempts have been made to identify a central dogma in Calvin's *Institutes* that is regulative of everything else, or even serves as the 'principle' from which everything else is deduced. Their failure has sometimes given rise to a forthright denial that Calvin was a systematic theologian at all. But the reaction is unwarranted. Calvin was manifestly concerned to see every part of his *Institutes* in the context of the whole; failure to take note of what is surely a systematic concern accounts for some of the mistakes that have plagued Calvin's critics and friends alike to this day. It is essential to ask, not simply what Calvin said on any given topic that happens to interest the reader, but also how it fits within the total design; and it is better to seek the links between topics in recurring metaphors rather than in some elusive central dogma.

God, humanity, and redemption 🌿

Calvin's thinking about God and God's relation to humanity is dominated by two favourite images: God is the fountain of good and the Father who cares for his children. The two images say the same thing, the one by a metaphor drawn from nature, the other by a metaphor from personal relationships: that whatever good we possess has its sole source in the abundant goodness of God. To acknowledge that this is so is what Calvin understands by piety, and where there is no piety we cannot properly say that God is known. The security of the 'pious' lies in their confidence 'that the heavenly Father so holds everything in his power . . . that nothing falls out unless by his design'.

The vocation of humanity—their unique role in the created order—is to render continual thanks to the Father and fountain of good. They live in the world as privileged spectators in a theatre of God's glory and accordingly should live in thankfulness, like mirrors reflecting the glory of God's goodness. But the shame of Adam was that he spurned the bounty God had lavished on him and so diminished God's glory. His descendants now sit like blind men in the theatre; they enjoy the gifts but do not see the hand of the giver. Calvin's remarks on human depravity offend our modern sensibilities. However, they do not express disgust with humanity, but rather with human ingratitude, which abandons piety for unbelief or transforms it into *impietas*, a servile dread of God that seeks to placate him with sacrifices.

Calvin perceives even *impietas*, though it is only a vain shadow of religion, as a confused knowledge of God. Hence the remedy, which is the word of God in scripture, can be compared to corrective lenses that assist our weak vision and focus our otherwise confused perception of God. Just how it was possible for Calvin to think of God's word as like a pair of spectacles is immediately clear from his understanding of the faith that receives it: faith is resting on the word of God's mercy or goodwill in Christ—that is, the gospel. Faith does what Adam's descendants can no longer do without the help of God's word: it recognizes God in his true character as the Father who means well to his children. Calvin can make the same point with his other favourite metaphor (in his *Commentary on John*, for example) when he speaks of Christ as the one who opens up access to the fountain. But the familial metaphor is particularly striking: often he simply identifies faith with the recognition of God's fatherhood, opposing it to the servile dread that God may be against us.

The cardinal Reformation doctrine of justification by faith is interpreted accordingly. It means that, being reconciled to God through Christ, we have a gracious Father in heaven instead of a judge. Calvin presents the passage from a servile to a filial consciousness of God most eloquently in his chapter on Christian freedom, which he introduces as an appendix to justification, intended to help us understand its 'power'. Servants, who are under the yoke of the law, are afraid to face their master unless they have done exactly what is demanded of them. But children do not hesitate to show their father unfinished projects that they have scarcely begun, or even have spoiled a little, confident that he will like them, 'however small, rough, or imperfect they may be'. The concept of 'merit' is thereby excluded. When scripture speaks of 'reward', it does not mean a servant's pay, but a child's inheritance.

It was Calvin's belief, however, that the grace of adoption was not for everyone. Scripture and experience concur that not all hear the gospel; and of those who do, not all receive it in faith. The difference between those who believe and those who do not cannot be attributed to human freedom without undermining the cardinal conviction that every good comes solely from the goodness or mercy of God, including the faith by which the gift of eternal life is received. Faith must be grounded wholly in God's freedom, not ours: there is an 'eternal election' by which God has predestined some to eternal life, others to destruction. As Calvin saw it, this election was the final, conclusive testimony to the utter gratuitousness of God's grace; hence it was also the foundation of both the assurance and the humility of the elect. Double predestination was not the centre of Calvin's theology, but it did qualify his understanding of the gospel: the restoration of humanity to prelapsarian piety was not intended for *all* humanity. Calvin's interest was in the recovery of Adamic piety, not in the fact (as he supposed it to be) that many would be excluded from it. But he was honest enough to admit that God's 'awe-inspiring decree' gives rise to 'great and difficult questions', which he tried energetically to answer from the scriptures, arguing that since no one deserves to be saved, God cannot be charged with injustice if he grants salvation to some and not to others.

The means of grace 🌿

The gift of faith is given through the word preached and made visible in the sacraments. Calvin attributes to preaching itself the kind of efficacy the medieval church ascribed to the sacraments. The word not only evokes faith; it is 'the instrument by which Jesus Christ, with all his graces, is dispensed to us'. But as adjuncts to the word the best of fathers has provided signs or figures of the grace that the word conveys: baptism is the sign of adoption into the Father's household; in the Lord's Supper (Eucharist) he gives his children a pledge of their continual nourishment with the bread of life, which is Jesus Christ. Both participate in the sacramental efficacy of the word.

Calvin's sacramental theology rested on Augustine's distinction between sign and reality. Luther had accused Huldrych Zwingli of misinterpreting Augustine, for whom a sign was the bearer of a present reality, not, as Zwingli thought, a reminder of something done in the past. Calvin's view was truer to Augustine's: though a sign is not itself the reality, it attests and brings the reality it signifies. The sign presents what it represents; if it were not so, God would be a deceiver. Such a sacramental theology posed obvious difficulties for an evangelical understanding of baptism, which is normally administered to infants. If salvation is by faith, how can an infant incapable of faith receive the grace that baptism signifies? The Calvinist teaching seemed to imply that there are, after all, two ways of being saved. Some even of Calvin's friends have doubted if he solved the problem. He insisted that baptism is administered only to the infant child of believing parents (in recognition of its birth within the covenant) and that it does require the future faith of the baptized if it is to become effective. But he did not hesitate to speak of infant regeneration as the sacrament's effect at the actual time of its administration.

In his teaching on the Eucharist Calvin became a leading advocate of the mediating position that emerged after the disastrous clash between the Lutherans and the Zwinglians at Marburg (1529). At a ground-breaking conference between Bucer and Melanchthon in December 1534, the bread and wine of the sacrament were identified as 'exhibitive' signs, 'which being proffered and taken, the body of Christ is proffered and taken at the same time' (Wittenberg Concord, art. 2). Calvin agreed. Since he rejected the Lutheran doctrine of the ubiquity of Christ's body, it was difficult for him to explain *how* communion with Christ's life-giving flesh takes place in the sacrament. He was content, he said, to feel what he could not understand. But from Romans 8: 9–11 he concluded that participation in Christ must be the work of the Holy Spirit. The sacramental signs are efficacious as the Spirit's 'instruments'. Though Calvin often used the language of simultaneity, according to which the reality is given *when* the sign is enacted, instrumentalism was more characteristic of him: the Spirit gives the reality *through* the sign.

Calvin devoted a chapter to what he perceived as the medieval perversion of the sacrament. The Lord's Supper, as the name implies, is a meal and not a sacrifice. It is indeed true that the body once offered on the cross is offered daily, but for nourishment not for propitiation: it is God's gift to the church, not the church's sacrifice to God. The

Roman mass did twofold violence to the sacrament: it turned the gift of God into a human work, and it dissolved the ecclesial community by reducing communion to the solitary deed of a priest. There is, to be sure, a eucharistic sacrifice since believers are consecrated by the sacrifice of Christ to an answering sacrifice of praise, which includes all the duties of love to their brothers and sisters. The sacrament is a liturgical enactment of this continual thanksgiving by God's people—a collective act of what Calvin understood by 'piety'. But it has nothing to do with appeasing God's anger.

The church and the civil government 🌿

Calvin's ideal was co-operation between church and state, each having its own constitution. But the dividing line between them was not wholly clear in principle, much less in practice. It is remarkable that civil government appears, alongside the church and the sacraments, under the general rubric 'The External Means or Aids by Which God Invites Us into the Society of Christ and Keeps Us Therein'. The civil magistrates are God's deputies; they occupy a holy office, which includes the responsibility of establishing true religion and preventing public blasphemies against God's truth. Their office extends to both tables of the Decalogue.

Perhaps because he saw the civil government as the institution responsible for the outward worship of God—public religion—Calvin spoke of the church mainly in terms of personal nurture. The church is the Mother of believers: as Cyprian said, having God for Father requires having the church for Mother. There is no other way to enter into life than for Mother Church to give us birth and care for us until we lay aside our mortal flesh and become like the angels. It is true that the church has the means for discipline as well as education and nurture in its fourfold ministry of pastors, teachers, elders, and deacons. But it is the civil government that wields a sword.

The significance of Calvinism for the political and economic institutions of the western world has been keenly debated. The questions are not in the main about Calvin's own opinions on economic and political affairs. His reflections on economic activity are mostly concerned to impose moral limits on the pursuit of monetary gain, not to encourage a free market. And the fact that his political ideas seem capable of development in opposite directions reflects his explicit intention to hold a middle course between those who renounce the civil order and the flatterers of princes, who praise their power too much.

Calvin's thoughts on civil government, summed up in the concluding chapter of the *Institutes*, were shaped by his location in republican Geneva and by his special concern for the Reformed minority in his native land; the use made of his political ideas was shaped in turn by the later fortunes of the Reformed churches both in and beyond France. His explicit point of departure in the chapter on church and state, however, is the characteristic assertion that the existence of the divinely ordained political order is yet another reason for gratitude to God. He has already (in book 3) invoked the 'two kingdoms' doctrine as a warning not to apply the gospel's teaching on spiritual freedom to the political order. In the chapter on civil government he now lays heavy emphasis on the duty of obedience to those in authority, even when their authority is abused: the obligation of subjects to obey is not contingent on the success with which rulers meet their obligation to rule for the good of their subjects.

It is true that Calvin shows himself suspicious of the absolute power of kings and expresses a preference either for aristocracy or for a mixed constitution in which not even the 'best men' have the sole voice. Hence he espouses the view that abuse of power at the highest level can and should be challenged by inferior magistrates if the existing constitution allows for it. Moreover, he believes that, as Daniel defied the edict of King Nebuchadnezzar (Dan. 6), even the private citizen who holds no constitutional office should not obey the civil government if obedience to human authority would mean disobedience to God. Plainly, however, there is no straight line from these qualifications of total passivity to the later Calvinist doctrines of active resistance and legitimate tyrannicide. Calvin thought subjects should be grateful if the form of government under which they lived was beneficent; but if not, they were to suffer it rather than attempt to change it. His horror of shedding the blood of the civil authorities, ordained as they were by God, prevented his views on the limits of compliance from ever becoming a defence of the right to armed resistance. The best the pious could do, whether lower magistrates or private citizens, was to hope that God would exercise the unique divine right of raising up an avenger to punish the injustice of the tyrant.

Calvin's intellectual legacy is not to be measured simply by his influence on western culture. His theology was first and foremost a contribution to Christian thought, and his achievement in the *Institutes* was his construction of a comprehensive interpretation of the Christian faith, an interpretation that continues to provide resources for theological construction today. Unfortunately, his achievement has been overshadowed by dislike of his personality and an obsessive preoccupation with a few issues—or even just one issue—torn from the total fabric of his thought. Calvin did not invent the practice of executing heretics. He had little if anything new to say on the Christian doctrine of election or predestination. The trial and execution of Servetus for denying the Trinity took place at a time when deviant believers were being put to death by the hundreds. And it is a serious failure of understanding when Calvin's treatment of election, which he placed at the end of the third book of the *Institutes*, is discussed with little regard for anything he has said before. The prominence of double predestination in later Calvinism tells us less about its place in Calvin's own thinking than about the points at which opponents outside and inside the Reformed church directed their sharpest criticisms.

Calvin's contribution to Christian thought can be fairly assessed only when seen as a whole. He stands in the company of such masters as Aquinas and Schleiermacher. Though he lacked the precision of the one and the originality of the other, his rhetorical style kept him closer than either of them to the immediate language of the believing community. To some, this may seem to be one of his special virtues.

Butin, Philip Walker, *Revelation, Redemption, and Response: Calvin's Trinitarian Understanding of the Divine Human Relationship* (1995).

Davis, Thomas J., *The Clearest Promises of God: The Development of Calvin's Eucharistic Teaching* (1995).

DeVries, Dawn, *Jesus Christ in the Preaching of Calvin and Schleiermacher* (1996).

Gerrish, B. A., *Grace and Gratitude: The Eucharistic Theology of John Calvin* (1993).

Hesselink, I. John, *Calvin's Concept of the Law* (1992).

Jones, Serene, *Calvin and the Rhetoric of Piety* (1995).

McGrath, Alister E., *A Life of John Calvin: A Study of the Shaping of Western Culture* (1990).

Parker, T. H. L., *Calvin: An Introduction to his Thought* (1995).

Puckett, David L., *John Calvin's Exegesis of the Old Testament* (1995).

Rainbow, Jonathan H., *The Will of God and the Cross: An Historical and Theological Study of John Calvin's Doctrine of Limited Redemption* (1990).

Schreiner, Susan E., *The Theater of His Glory: Nature and the Natural Order in the Thought of John Calvin* (1991).

—— *Where Shall Wisdom Be Found? Calvin's Exegesis of Job from Medieval and Modern Perspectives* (1994).

Steinmetz, David C., *Calvin in Context* (1995).

Tamburello, Dennis E., *Union With Christ: John Calvin and the Mysticism of St. Bernard* (1994).

Zachman, Randall C., *The Assurance of Faith: Conscience in the Theology of Martin Luther and John Calvin* (1993).

X

Blaise Pascal (1623–1662)

NICHOLAS HAMMOND

A French mathematician, scientist, religious polemicist, and apologist, Pascal was born in Clermont-Ferrand, the son of Étienne Pascal, a high-ranking officer in the fiscal bureaucracy of the area. His mother died when he was 3, and his father undertook the education of Blaise and his two sisters, Gilberte and Jacqueline, especially after 1631 when the family moved to Paris. Pascal showed precocious scientific skills, which continued in Rouen where his father was appointed tax commissioner for Normandy in 1639. In 1646, two Jansenist brothers treated Étienne Pascal for a broken hip, which resulted in the whole family converting to Jansenism. This episode is sometimes known as Pascal's 'first conversion'. In 1647, Pascal secured the condemnation of a former Capuchin, Jacques Forton (Frère Saint-Ange), who had maintained that reason played an important role in the mysteries of faith. Leaving Rouen in 1648, the family eventually settled in Paris, where Pascal was an active participant in scientific circles. Amongst Pascal's achievements as a scientist in Rouen and Paris are his treatises on conical sections, vacuums, and the arithmetical triangle, as well as the invention of a calculating machine. In 1651, after the death of Étienne

Pascal, Jacqueline entered the convent at Port-Royal, against her brother's wishes. On 23 November 1654, Pascal underwent a definitive conversion, known as his 'second conversion', the experience of which he recorded in a document known as the 'Memorial' which he kept sewn into his clothing for the remainder of his life. After this time, Pascal was a frequent visitor to Port-Royal. From 1658 until his death, he was plagued by ill health. Two works in particular distinguish Pascal as a Christian thinker, the *Lettres provinciales* (*Provincial Letters*) and the *Pensées*.

The *Provincial Letters* appeared initially as a series of pamphlets between January 1656 and June 1657, and were published together as eighteen letters in 1657, under the pseudonym of Louis de Montalte. Pascal's decision to write anonymously resulted from the acrimonious dispute between two leading Catholic parties, the Jesuits (who had the support of the King, Louis XIV) and the Jansenists, named after the Flemish theologian and bishop of Ypres, Cornelius Jansenius, who were based at Port-Royal convent in Paris, and whom Pascal was trying to defend.

The posthumous publication of Jansenius's *Augustinus* (1640), which constituted an attempt to vindicate the teaching of Augustine against the more recent Jesuit theologians, provoked a debate between a leading theologian at Port-Royal, Antoine Arnauld, and the Sorbonne. Arnauld was about to be censured for taking a stand on five so-called heretical propositions which were allegedly to be found in the *Augustinus*. Because of the risk of imprisonment which Port-Royal sympathizers ran if they were discovered to be attacking the Jesuits, Pascal, who at that time was known only for his mathematical and scientific talents, was chosen to defend Arnauld. The resulting letters, written with the freshness and immediacy of someone not trained in theological intricacies, both appealed to and were understandable by a wider secular audience. Through the use of an interview technique and the selective quotation of Jesuit writers, Pascal manages to make the

Jesuits condemn themselves out of their own mouths, which is exacerbated by the comic juxtaposition of an excitable and buffoon-like Jesuit central figure and a quietly reasonable Jansenist. Perhaps the greatest *tour de force* of the early letters is Pascal's ability to maintain the general reader's interest in a complex debate that is focused largely on the Jesuits' use of terms such as 'proximate power' and 'sufficient grace'. Pascal strongly opposed the Jesuit position that all human beings have *sufficient* grace in them to be saved. The Jansenists believed, on the contrary, that efficacious grace is reserved only for a select few and that this grace cannot be misused. Pascal had elaborated these ideas in his *Écrits sur la grâce (Writings on Grace*, written *c.*1657–8), in which he contrasts the Calvinist, Jesuit, and Jansenist views on grace.

The *Pensées*, left unfinished at Pascal's death and first published in 1670, is the work which marks Pascal above all as a Christian apologist. As the incomplete text comprised various classified and unclassified bundles, the uncertain ordering of the fragments has resulted in numerous editions of the *Pensées*, each with different numbering. There are strong indications that Pascal was intending to give the work a very different structure from that of preceding writers' works, as he reiterates that, whereas his subject-matter has often been treated by others, 'the ordering is new'. Written in order to try and persuade the sceptics and non-believers of Pascal's time of the necessity for religious belief, this collection of fragments and longer passages is still widely read by Christians and non-Christians alike. Many of the fragments, while appearing to be reflections on the human condition without direct reference to Christian thought, are none the less imbued with an Augustinian pessimism that points always to mankind's post-lapsarian corrupt state.

One of the most famous passages, known as the Wager, is perceived by many to foreshadow 20th-century existentialist writers in the discussion of free will and commitment. Although the Wager has often been interpreted erroneously as a mathematical attempt to prove the existence of God, mathematical proofs are demonstrated finally to be inadequate in the realm of religious persuasion. Instead, the reader is shown to be involuntarily involved in the game of wagering either for or against God's existence, as indifference or uncertainty is deemed by Pascal to be akin to betting against God. As the main speaker in the fragment tells his interlocutor, 'you must wager; there is no choice, you are already committed'. Although reason is seen by Pascal to be a sign of man's greatness, he nevertheless strongly opposes Descartes's belief that human reason alone can comprehend God. According to Pascal, this view does not take into account the role of intuition (called 'the heart' by Pascal) in religious faith, as is evident in another fragment: 'the heart has its reasons that reason cannot know.'

Amongst other longer sections from the *Pensées* that deal directly with the Christian faith, in the fragment known as the Disproportion of Man Pascal makes use of recent scientific discoveries (such as the invention of the telescope and the microscope) to show the contradictions of the human condition. In a world where we find ourselves to be both tiny entities in contrast to the vastness of space and enormous when compared to minute organisms undetectable to the human eye, it is inevitable that we should be in a state of uncertainty, somewhere 'between everything and nothing', as he describes it. Another longer passage is known as the Mystery of Jesus, where Christ is imagined in the Garden of Gethsemane speaking both to his disciples and to an unnamed interlocutor.

Those passages which deal directly with non-believers show Pascal's psychological manipulation of his reader, where often a sceptical interlocutor is flattered before being attacked. Nor is Pascal afraid to use strongly emotive imagery to portray the human condition, as in the fragment where human beings in a godless world are portrayed as prisoners in chains awaiting inevitable death. The terror of the non-believer at the enormity of the universe is captured eloquently in the famous line, 'the eternal silence of these infinite spaces terrifies me'.

Other pieces within the *Pensées* concern historical proofs of Christ, prophecies, and miracles.

Pascal's work encompasses many paradoxes, which makes it impossible to place him in simple categories. Such paradoxes include the fact that, while his scientific work showed his willingness to embrace new and radical ideas, he remained a theological and political conservative. Moreover, although he subscribed to the rigorous Augustinianism of the Jansenists, he still absorbed the writings of secular writers such as Montaigne and Epictetus in his own work, as is evident in the record of his discussions with his spiritual director, *Conversation with M. de Sacy* (*c*.1655). Perhaps most tellingly, Pascal often uses such contradictions to add weight to his arguments. In the *Pensées*, for example, he redirects his initial condemnation of such matters as Imagination, Custom, Diversion, and even Self-love to show their positive use. Pascal has rightly been seen as an innovative Christian thinker whose influence transcends narrow boundaries. Both his ability to introduce complex issues to a lay audience in a readily comprehensible way and his attempt to understand the psychology of his intended readers make him memorable (in a manner that many of his contemporary religious writers were not) and approachable to a modern readership.

Pascal, B., *Pensées*, trans. A. J. Krailsheimer (1966).
—— *Provincial Letters*, trans. A. J. Krailsheimer (1967).
—— *Pensées*, trans. H. Levi (1995).
Davidson, H. M., *Blaise Pascal* (1983).
Hammond, N., *Playing with Truth: Language and the Human Condition in Pascal's* Pensées (1994).
Krailsheimer, A. J., *Pascal* (1980).
Mesnard, J., *Les Pensées de Pascal*, 2nd edn. (1991).
Norman, B., *Portraits of Thought: Knowledge, Methods and Styles in Pascal* (1988).
Parish, R. J., *Pascal's* Lettres provinciales: *A Study in Polemic* (1989).
Rex, W. E., *Pascal's Provincial Letters: An Introduction* (1977).

Sellier, P., *Pascal et saint Augustin*, 2nd edn. (1995).

Wetsel, D., *Pascal and Disbelief: Catechesis and Conversion in the* Pensées (1994).

XI

Jonathan Edwards (1703-1758)

CAROLINE SCHRÖDER

Edwards is considered by some the greatest theologian of the 18th century. The leading preacher and champion of the First Great Awakening, Edwards wrote works on theology, philosophy, and ethics aimed at upholding Christian orthodoxy in the age of the Enlightenment. He was born in East Windsor, Connecticut, and educated from 1716 to 1720 at Yale. Having spent a short time serving a small Presbyterian congregation in New York, he returned to Yale as a tutor. In 1727 he married Sarah Pierrepont from New Haven; they had eleven children. In the same year, Edwards began his ministry in Northampton, Massachusetts, first as assistant to his ageing grandfather, the influential Solomon Stoddard, and later as sole minister; it ended with his unfortunate dismissal in 1750. The following years (1751-7) were spent in Stockbridge, a frontier settlement at the western edge of Massachusetts, where Edwards was in charge of a small community of white settlers and of the local mission to a Houssatonic band. In 1757 he was voted president of the College of New Jersey in Princeton. He had some hesitation in accepting the offer, for his years in Stockbridge, initially a kind of exile, had become very productive. Here he had written his major philosophical works, including *Freedom of the Will* and *The Nature of True Virtue*. He had hoped to work on a more systematic account of Christian doctrine. But only a few weeks after his departure from Stockbridge and his induction as president he died as the result of a smallpox inoculation.

In Edwards's boyhood he had been fascinated by 'flying spiders'. Years after recording his observations of them, he used the spider-image in his most famous sermon, 'Sinners in the Hands of an Angry God', preached at Enfield, Connecticut, in 1741. The dangling spider represented the unconverted sinner hanging over the pit of hell. The resulting sense of imminent threat is intensified when one discovers that God is both one's enemy and one's saviour. Edwards forces his congregation to see itself, unbearably, as without Christ: in the midst of death, held only by the slender thread of life, which is no more than God's temporary restraint of his will to leave the sinner to eternal destruction. But despite Edwards's determination to confront his contemporaries with the shattering reality of the will of God, he was not a typical revivalist. The moderate style of his preaching, the depth of his thought and its wide horizon distinguish him from such itinerant preachers as George Whitefield and James Davenport, whose charismatic impact left their audiences fired with religious enthusiasm. Unfortunately, later generations seem to have had selective memories: they remembered and abhorred Edwards as preaching hellfire sermons, and affirming God in a way that diminishes humanity. Both his opponents and his friends have created him according to their own ideas. He is seen as the tragic hero of an outmoded European Calvinism, or, on the contrary, as an early example of new, modern America: sometimes as the father of transcendentalism, sometimes even as belonging to the world of postmodernity. Some of his writings, such as the *Life of David Brainerd*, *A Faithful Narrative*, *Religious Affections*, and *A History of the Work of Redemption*, made a strong impact on 19th-century evangelicalism, with its interest in mission, its millennialist hopes, and its emphasis on personal sanctification. Questions about Edwards's personal life preoccupied a number of scholars. His private notes, the *Miscellanies*, edited by Thomas Schafer, were expected to reveal some secret about a man whose thoughts and writings often looked like pieces of a puzzle that did not fit together.

In *God Glorified in Man's Dependence*, his first sermon to be published, Edwards expresses what was to be central to his theology: God's sovereignty, not matched by any human effort. His emphasis on the asymmetry and immediacy of the relationship between God and the human being was puzzling to an audience accustomed to the mediating arrangements of covenant theology. The sermon expresses another aspect of Edwards's theological realism: faith is a sense of what is real in the work of redemption, which later helped him to steer the vessel of religious experience between the Scylla and Charybdis of Antinomianism and Arminianism.

In *A Divine and Supernatural Light* we encounter the keyword of Edwards's religious psychology: the gift of a new 'sense'. He shows a mystical tendency in favouring the metaphor of light. What a truly religious person knows is beyond notional knowledge, being based on an experience similar to an actual sensation. It is an immediate grasp of the beauty of God's work of redemption, and is more effectual than reason or education in disposing human beings to accept it. In short: true religion is a matter of the heart and its affections, but the human heart tends to self-deception and hypocrisy, so affections which claim to be religious must be tested by a number of reasonable criteria. *Religious Affections*, Edwards's last defence of the Awakening against growing criticism, is impressive evidence of his unwillingness to reduce religion to an emotionalism that encourages people to rely solely on their own 'extraordinary' experiences and immunizes them against questioning by the community of the church.

Edwards inherited from his grandfather Solomon Stoddard a set of problems focused on the church as the visible community of saints.

Originally only the children of church members were admitted to baptism, and to be accepted as a member one was expected to undergo and publicly declare some kind of conversion experience. There was a great deal of uncertainty about the nature of this experience and the accounts given of it before the congregation. Conversion can simply be seen as the moment when the Christian doctrine of salvation is taken personally: whereas up till now I have been a more or less indifferent member of the audience, I now discover myself as an actor in the drama itself. According to the ecclesiology of 'visible saints', a minister's primary responsibility was the pastoral care of those still only in the audience, who needed to be guided into the story of salvation. Now came the questions to which Edwards, like any other minister of the Puritan tradition, had to find answers: Is there such a thing as guidance? Does people's experience of conversion follow a fixed pattern? Are there any steps we can take preparatory to that life-changing moment when saving faith first emerges? Do we know anything about human nature that helps us to initiate the process? From his own experience, Edwards knew that all these pastoral efforts towards stimulating conversion were misleading. When the first revivals occurred in his parish in 1734, he understood them as God's own testimony to the doctrine of justification by faith alone. The beginning of the Awakening in Northampton can be seen as the first blow struck against the compromise of the Half-way Covenant, with its tacit implication that public and visible religion is simply morality. The Half-way Covenant, introduced in 1662 and favoured by Stoddard and many others, allowed the children of the growing number of unconverted parents to be baptized: parents who could not claim any conversion experience were treated as people sincerely longing for true religion and therefore on their way into the church. But the Awakening proclaimed that there is no area for 'half-way-Christians'. The middle ground between world and church, the distance between 'total depravity' and true religion, cannot be measured. It is God's immediate presence that creates something entirely new, both in personal and in public life, and invalidates all the means by which we order and manipulate our lives before God and our fellow human beings.

In *Freedom of the Will* Edwards declares that the only freedom necessary for human beings to be considered moral agents is freedom in the sense that one is able to do as one wills: that one's behaviour is a coherent expression of who one is. People are free to behave as they are, not free to choose who and what they are: their nature, habits, and inclinations are part of the biography given to them before and beyond any specific act of will. Hence his controversial achievement was to establish a concept of human freedom by which a person is seen as both totally dependent upon God's providence and fully consistent with her own nature. The expression of that freedom, emphasizing both determinism and responsibility, was the ambiguous notion of 'moral necessity' as the basic structure of human life in general, and one of the few qualities that the regenerate and unregenerate have in common.

Edwards's purpose was to show that a certain religious liberalism had taken root in American soil, which undermined the doctrinal fortress built in 1618 by the Synod of Dort to protect the sovereignty of God and its foremost expression, the doctrine of predestination, against the Arminians. He opts for an anthropology of total depravity both in *Original Sin*, and in the *The Nature of True Virtue*, in which he exposes humanity's moral capabilities before regeneration, however impressive, as inconceivably distant from the true beauty of a spiritual and virtuous life. He stands for 'unconditional election', questions the meaning of preparation, and interprets the Awakening as God's testimony to the doctrine of justification by faith alone. We find him holding on to the doctrine of 'limited atonement' when he addresses his congregation with the urgency of a revivalist for whom the final division of humankind into two irreconcilable camps is a given and indisputable fact. We see him alluding to John Locke's 'simple idea' in support of the tenet of 'irresistible grace' and comparing religious experience with the supernatural gift of a new sense. Finally, we see his increasing concern for the 'perseverance of the saints' when he insists that good dispositions and works spring from faith as good fruit grows on a good tree. When the revivalist preacher loses his initial naivety and becomes a critic of the Awakening in general and of his congregation in particular, he is responding to people's self-centred interest in sensational experiences exalting them above the duties of their daily unobtrusive lives. True religion is not one among many aspects of human reality. It disrupts the hopeless habits of a person's and a society's life, in ways that human beings cannot foresee as the millennium breaks through the structures of history. But it needs to be more than a mountain-peak experience of incommunicable emotions. That experience demands expression in intelligible words and in a life that can be recognized as according with what the church knows of the will of God.

Cherry, C., *The Theology of Jonathan Edwards. A Reappraisal*, new edn. (1990).

Conforti, J. A., *Jonathan Edwards: Religious Tradition, and American Culture from the Second Great Awakening to the Twentieth Century* (1995).

Fiering, N. S., *Jonathan Edwards's Moral Thought and its British Context* (1981).

Guelzo, A. C., *Edwards on the Will: A Century of American Theological Debate* (1989).

Jenson, R. W., *America's Theologian: A Recommendation of Jonathan Edwards* (1988)

Lee, S. H., *The Philosophical Theology of Jonathan Edwards* (1988).

Lesser, M. X., *Jonathan Edwards* (1988).

—— *Jonathan Edwards: An Annotated Bibliography, 1979–1993* (1994).

Miller, P., *Jonathan Edwards* (1949).

—— **and Smith, J. E.** (eds.), *The Works of Jonathan Edwards* (1957–   ).

Murray, I. H., *Jonathan Edwards. A New Biography* (1987).

Schroeder, C., *Glaubenswahrnehmung und Selbsterkenntnis: Jonathan Edwards's* theologia experimentalis (1998).

Stein, S. J. (ed.), *Jonathan Edwards's Writings: Text, Context, Interpretation* (1996).

XII

Immanuel Kant (1724–1804)

JOHN E. HARE

The question of Kant's relation to Christianity has been controversial from his own time to the present. While the view offered in this article is responsible to the texts, there is no consensus among Kant scholars. He nowhere tells us about his personal religious beliefs, for example whether he believed that Christ rose from the dead. He does, however, tell us that certain religious beliefs are required for the practice of the moral life, and others are 'vehicles' by which moral faith is transmitted to us. Sometimes interpreters talk of Kant as being tactful about Christianity, disguising his distaste to appease the Prussian authorities, but a more straightforward approach is adopted here.

Kant grew up in a pietist Lutheran family, and had pietist Lutheran schooling. We need to read his work, especially in the philosophy of religion, as constantly engaged in discussion with Pietism. Comparing Kant with one of its great figures, August Hermann Francke, reveals that both emphasize the primacy of practice over theory in the life of faith. Both change the emphasis from history to what God wants to do in every human heart. Both insist that we have no natural ability to destroy the root of evil in our souls. Both distrust the natural inclinations, but think they can be trained to serve God either directly or indirectly. Finally, both have the vision of a worldwide moral and spiritual renewal, and think of the visible church as a potential hindrance to this. But Kant also defined himself in some ways in opposition to the pietists. He was against what he calls 'fanaticism', and objected to the claims some pietists made to being supernaturally favoured by God. 'To claim that we *feel* as such the immediate influence of God is self-contradictory, because the Idea of God lies only in reason.' Kant did not attend religious services, even as rector of the university, perhaps because of his experience of Christianity's tendency to become what he calls 'dictatorial'. But this opposition to Pietism is also characteristic of Lutheranism in his day, though of a different branch. Kant's combination is idiosyncratic; but, without further evidence, we should not place him outside Christian orthodoxy.

In the *Critique of Pure Reason*, Kant argues that we cannot, on his restrictive view of knowledge, *know* that God exists; for we could not possibly experience his existence with the senses. God is a thing-in-itself, a *noumenon*, beyond the range of our sensory intuition of *phenomena*. Accordingly he criticized the traditional proofs of God's existence—such as the ontological, cosmological, and teleological arguments—as overstepping the limits of the human understanding. This is part of Kant's 'Copernican revolution'. Copernicus had suggested that we could understand our observations of the movements of the heavenly bodies as a function of our own movement. In the same way, Kant suggests that we can see the a priori principles of human knowledge as a function of the limits to which our sense-experience has to conform. But pointing to human limits does not, for Kant, imply scepticism. He wants to limit knowledge to make room for faith. In the *Critique of Practical Reason* he argues that we have to *believe* that God exists, because we continue throughout our lives to desire our own happiness in everything else that we desire. There is nothing wrong here. What is wrong is our inborn condition in which we put the desire for our own happiness *above* the desire to do our duty. If by some revolution of the will this priority can be reversed, we shall still be desiring our own happiness. Hence if we are to persevere in the moral life, we have to believe that it is consistent with our own happiness: that we do not have to do what is morally wrong in order to be happy. This is not the justification for the moral life, for that would turn it into a means towards happiness; whereas we should do our duty for its own sake. But we do have to believe that our attempts at virtue are rewarded by happiness, which in turn requires us to believe in someone who can do the rewarding, namely God. Kant has a similar argument for the need to believe in personal immortality. The moral law requires us to be committed in this life to the pursuit of holiness. But we do not see such a pursuit even near to fulfilment in this life, and to sustain our endeavour we need to believe that the pursuit can be continued in the next. Finally, in the *Critique of Judgement*, he argues that reason has to ask why nature exists, and cannot answer without imagining a being who, in creating nature, gave it an ultimate end.

We should think of our duties as God's commands. God is the head of the kingdom of ends, and we are members in this same kingdom. In this kingdom of ends, we treat all other rational beings as ends in themselves, not as mere means to our ends. To treat another person as an end in herself is to make her ends our own ends, as far as the moral law allows. The kingdom of which God is head is thus a system of morally permissible ends shared by all rational agents. The possible realization of this kingdom (required for its normativity) is produced by God's headship of it, just as in the political realm the possible realization of the *polis* (again required for its normativity) is produced by the exercise of political authority. There is, in our relation both to God and to political authority, an autonomous submission, which is not liable to Kant's objections to heteronomy. Heteronomy means making something other than our respect for the moral law (for example, fear of punishment) the ground of our action. Kant thought that some pietist versions of divine command theory were guilty of this, but that his own view, that we should see our duties as God's commands, is not.

Kant's relation to the bible is an area in which his interpreters disagree. Some call him a deist, in the sense that he does not accept special revelation. It is better to take him, in his own term, as a 'pure rationalist': he accepts special revelation but does not think this acceptance necessary to rational religion. In the prologue to the second edition of *Religion within the Limits of Reason Alone*, he suggests that we see revelation as two concentric circles. The historical revelation (to particular people at particular times) lies in the outer circle; the revelation to reason (which Kant takes not to be historical in this sense, but the same in all people at all times) lies in the inner one. He then takes the central items of the historical revelation (creation, Fall, redemption, and Second Coming), to see if they can be translated into the language of the inner circle in the light of moral concepts. Since Kant is a pure rationalist, we can expect him, by this translation, to demonstrate the consistency of the historical faith with the religion of pure reason, but also to deny that the historical faith is the only possible way to reach a saving faith. He thinks it possible to lead a life sufficient for God to decree salvation even though it is lived outside the geographical and historical reach of the Christian scriptures. But for Kant himself and his contemporaries in Christian Europe, the Christian scriptures have been the 'vehicle' of saving faith.

Despite being a pure rationalist, Kant also concedes that we may have to believe some item in the outer circle, even though we cannot make use of it with our reason either theoretically or practically. An important case is raised by what he calls 'Spener's problem', referring to the great pietist and his treatment of the Christian doctrine of original sin. According to Spener we are born with the disposition not to love God with all our hearts, minds, souls, and strength and not to love our neighbours as ourselves. Nor can we get ourselves out of this disposition by our own devices. Spener's problem was how, given this incapacity, we can change; 'how we can become *other* men and not merely better men (as if we were already good but only negligent about the degree of our goodness).' Kant agrees with Spener (and Luther) that human beings are born in bondage to radical evil: in Kant's terms, with an innate tendency to prefer our own happiness to our duty. But then how can we change to the opposite preference, as required by morality? Kant thinks that 'ought' implies 'can'; if we cannot live under the moral law, then it is not the case that we ought to do so. But he is sure that we ought, and therefore he has to be able to assert that we can. He concedes, however, that we cannot bring about by our own devices the required revolution of the will. In his terms, the propensity to evil is radical, and is therefore inextirpable by human powers, 'since extirpation could occur only through good maxims, and cannot take place when the ultimate subjective ground of all maxims is postulated as corrupt'. This is Spener's problem. And Kant's solution is also Spener's; he appeals to divine assistance. We must believe that it is God who works in us, by negative and positive helps, to bring about the revolution of the will. 'Ought' implies 'can'; but 'ought' does not imply 'can by our own devices'. What we can accomplish depends upon what kind of assistance is available to us. This doctrine of the availability of divine grace is both something Kant thinks we have to accept if we are to sustain the moral life and something he cannot translate without remainder into the language of the inner circle.

Kant's philosophy of religion has been immensely influential. The greatest influence has been from the Copernican revolution, and the accompanying project of reconciling science and moral life. The influence goes through Hegel (who saw himself, like Luther, as a reformer of Christianity) and Kierkegaard (who repeats, in the figure of Judge William, Kant's translations of Christian doctrine into ethical terms). In Christian theology, Schleiermacher (to mention only the most important name of the nineteenth century) was deeply immersed in Kant, as were in the twentieth century Otto, Tillich, and Barth (though all three partially define themselves in opposition to him). The liberal Protestantism of Ritschl was also neo-Kantian in inspiration. In philosophy, the influence can be felt both in the Continental tradition, through Nietzsche and Heidegger, and in the analytic tradition through Russell and Austin. It is interesting to see how secular the Kantian tradition becomes even though in Kant himself there are still strong moorings in Christianity. His reconciliation project, together with its Christian basis, is widely perceived to have failed. This author believes that the project is bound to fail when detached, as it has been, from its traditional base; but this cannot be argued here.

Kant, I., *Practical Philosophy*, ET (1996).

—— *Religion and Rational Theology*, ET (1996).

—— *Critique of Pure Reason*, ET (1956).

—— *Critique of Judgement*, ET (1987).

Hare, John E., *The Moral Gap: Kantian Ethics, Human Limits, and God's Assistance* (1996).

Michalson, Gordon, *Fallen Freedom: Kant on Radical Evil and Moral Regeneration* (1990).

Reardon, Bernard M. G., *Kant as Philosophical Theologian* (1988).

Rossi, Philip J., and Wreen, Michael (eds.), *Kant's Philosophy of Religion Reconsidered* (1991).

Schneewind, Jerome, *The Invention of Autonomy* (1998).

Wood, Allen W., *Kant's Moral Religion* (1970).

—— *Kant's Rational Theology* (1978).

XIII

Friedrich Daniel Ernst Schleiermacher (1768–1834)

B. A. Gerrish

The German Protestant thinker Schleiermacher is commonly acclaimed 'the father of modern theology'. Schleiermacher's books and unpublished manuscripts range widely over the various philosophical disciplines and every branch of theological studies except Old Testament. He was also an influential public figure through his pulpit in the Trinity Church, Berlin, and has earned high regard for his translations of Plato's dialogues, thoughts on education, and pioneering work in hermeneutics. His chief importance for Christian thought lies in his attempt to set the study of theology on a new footing at a time when the problem was no longer the existence of errors and abuses in the church, as in the Reformation era, but rather the alienation of the modern world from the entire Christian tradition.

Schleiermacher lived the problem of faith and modernity in his own pilgrimage. Born into a family of Reformed (Calvinistic) preachers, he was sent to a Moravian school, where he underwent a conversion and learned the love for the Saviour that lay at the heart of Moravian Pietism. When he moved on to the Moravian seminary, his enquiring mind began to doubt what his teachers told him of Christ's deity and vicarious punishment for sin. What he lost, however, was not his faith in Christ, but his first interpretation of it. He dropped out of the seminary and transferred to the University of Halle, once the home of Pietism but for many years a stronghold of rationalism. Nevertheless, he completed his study for the ministry of the Reformed Church, and a return visit to the Moravian community later drew from him an intriguing testimony: 'I may say that I have become, after all, a pietist again, only of a higher order.'

From apologetics to church dogmatics 🌿

Schleiermacher's first book, often said to have inaugurated the modern period in Christian thought, appeared anonymously in 1799, when he was Reformed chaplain at the Charité Hospital in Berlin. A work of Christian apologetics, *On Religion: Speeches to its Cultured Despisers*, was written at the urging of his friends, many of whom were disdainful of the church. Since they shared his dislike of eighteenth century rationalism and moralism, his strategy was to persuade them that their move from the Enlightenment to Romanticism actually made them, 'however unintentionally, the rescuers and cherishers of religion'. But what is religion? To answer, Schleiermacher began on the inside: not with the outward trappings of dogma and usages that his friends despised, but with what he took to be a universal, if elusive, element in every human consciousness, including the consciousness of religion's cultured despisers. Religion is something antecedent to beliefs and dogmas, which only arise out of second-order reflection on religion.

In the second of the five speeches, Schleiermacher argued that the essence of religion, disclosed to the inward glance of introspection, is 'sense and taste for the Infinite'. He did not mean the Infinite merely as the endless multiplicity of finite things, but rather as the boundless underlying unity that makes the universe a whole. We cannot see or know this unity any more than we can see or know the universe as the sum total of finite existents. The One in the All is accessible only to feeling. To be religious, then, is to feel that everything that affects us is, at bottom, one: which is to say, that our being and living are a being and living through God. We cannot argue that God is needed as an item in our scientific knowledge of the world, nor that religion provides us with the moral duties requisite to being good citizens. And yet the scientific enterprise fills its sails from the sense of the Infinite, the One in the All, and religion accompanies every human deed like sacred music. In short, religion is an indispensable 'third' in being human, alongside knowing and doing, and the humanity the Romantics so eagerly cultivated is diminished whenever religion is neglected or despised.

From the second speech one could easily infer that Schleiermacher's religion was individualistic and mystical. The inference might not be corrected even by a reading of the fourth speech, in which religious community is reduced to mutual exchange between religious individuals. But the final speech discloses that the essence of religion described in speech two is only an abstraction from the concrete mode in which religion actually exists in any society or individual. Introspection tells us what religion is, but not how we have it: we have religion only in the religions. Schleiermacher's apology accordingly reaches its final goal with the case for Christianity as the best we have yet witnessed in the world's great historical religions.

After a brief tenure as professor and university preacher at the University of Halle, Schleiermacher returned to Berlin, where he became Reformed pastor at the Trinity Church (1809) and concurrently (from 1810) professor of theology at the new university. In 1821–2 appeared the second main work on which his reputation as a Christian thinker chiefly rests: *The Christian Faith, Presented Systematically According to the Principles of the Evangelical Church*. Despite the reservations he had expressed in the *Speeches* about 'systems', the two-volume *Christian Faith* is a tight, comprehensive work of systematic theology. More precisely, its genre is church dogmatics. In his

Brief Outline of the Study of Theology (1811; 2nd edn., 1830), Schleiermacher offered a classification of the various disciplines requisite for the preparation of church leaders. Surprisingly, he located dogmatics under 'historical theology', which is carefully distinguished from 'philosophical' and 'practical' theology and includes (besides dogmatics) exegetical theology and church history. He also divided dogmatics itself into *Glaubenslehre* (Christian doctrine) and *Sittenlehre* (Christian ethics). *The Christian Faith* is a work of *Glaubenslehre*, the science of faith. Unfortunately, the companion work on *Sittenlehre*, the science of morals, was not completed or published in Schleiermacher's lifetime.

Because present-day use of the term 'theology' is much less precise than his, Schleiermacher's careful division of the total field of theological study may strike us as fussy. But for two closely connected reasons it is crucial to a proper understanding of what he was doing in his dogmatic masterwork. First, *The Christian Faith* does not present the whole of Schleiermacher's theology, but only one division of his dogmatics. Dogmatic theology is not apologetic or philosophical theology (as he understood it). It is not practical theology, immediately transferable to the pulpit, even though it exists solely for the sake of preaching. It is not exegetical theology, which Schleiermacher took to be a co-ordinate discipline distinct from dogmatics. It is always possible to raise on exegetical grounds the question whether a dogmatic proposition is *Christian*. But dogmatics is concerned with the faith of a particular Christian community at the present time, and no Christian community is ever a mere replica of the apostolic age. Hence the subtitle of *The Christian Faith* states: 'according to the principles of the evangelical church.' Schleiermacher means the Evangelical Church of the Prussian Union—his own church, created by union of the Lutherans and the Reformed. The dogmatic question, for him, is whether a proposition is soundly evangelical. And it is this conception of the particularity of the dogmatic task that led Schleiermacher, secondly, to classify the discipline as 'historical'. Its object of enquiry is something that inevitably undergoes temporal change: not immutable dogma, but the living faith of a particular Christian community, or the way the community has brought the NT norm to bear on its own particular situation and expressed its faith in distinctive creeds or confessions.

Believing that the critical reception of his *Glaubenslehre* (as he liked to call it) was marred by misunderstandings, Schleiermacher paved the way for a new edition (1830–1) with two 'open letters' in a leading theological journal (1829). He was astonished that *The Christian Faith* had been widely read and judged as a philosophical work, a marshalling of proofs and concepts to support a general religiousness and a brave attempt to salvage whatever could be salvaged of church doctrines by assimilating them to a pantheistic philosophy. He insisted, in reply, that the actual aim of the work was to describe the distinctively Christian consciousness. Christians bear their entire consciousness of God as something brought about in them by Christ. Properly so called, Christianity is nothing other than faith in a revelation of God in the person of Jesus. Schleiermacher's aim, therefore, was to describe the need for redemption and its satisfaction through Christ as actual facts of experience. Of course, it was his intention to present Christian faith more particularly in one of the specific forms it had taken (in the Prussian church). Further, Schleiermacher expressly stated his persuasion that every dogma that represents a genuine element in the Christian consciousness can be so conceived as to avoid conflict with natural and historical science. This, too, belongs to his dogmatic programme. But the substance of the programme outlined in the letters is given as proposition 19 of the new edition of *The Christian Faith*: 'Dogmatic theology is the science of the system of doctrine generally accepted in a Christian church at a given time.' Such a science is not designed to prove the truth of Christian faith. It can only be pursued from within the believing community. For this reason, Schleiermacher set on the title page of *The Christian Faith* epigraphs from Anselm, ending with the words: 'Anyone who has not experienced will not understand.'

Leading themes in Schleiermacher's dogmatics 🌿

Schleiermacher's *Christian Faith* traverses the entire territory of the inherited Protestant dogmatics. But his main concern was to give an account of the distinctively Christian consciousness of sin and grace, the overall theme of the second part of the work. Original sin is not the state into which Adam and Eve fell from their created innocence: the doctrines of original perfection (discussed in part one) and original sin are not about two successive stages in the lives of the first human pair, but about two possibilities that coexist in the human nature of every man and every woman. There is the possibility of being conscious of God in every moment, and there is the possibility that the consciousness of God will be inhibited by the lower or sensible self-consciousness in its commerce with the finite objects of daily existence. The strength of the sensible self-consciousness comes partly from the fact that in each of us it develops first; the God-consciousness emerges later, and only fitfully. There is no progressive ascendancy of the spirit over the flesh. To be sure, the capacity for consciousness of God, which belongs to the *original perfection* of human nature, is never annulled, or else the relative impotence of the God-consciousness could hardly become 'sin', something for which we acknowledge responsibility. And yet, in agreement with the dogmatic tradition, Schleiermacher holds that in all of us there is a sinfulness that has its ground outside individuals, in the common life of sinful humanity into which they are born. This, then, is how we are to understand the *original sin* (German *Erbsünde*, 'inherited sin') that subjects us to a complete incapacity for good, from which we can be set free only by redemption. Actual sin is our voluntary perpetuation of what we thus inherit.

Schleiermacher's treatment of sin is a subtle interweaving of the old Reformation themes of bondage and responsibility. Here, as elsewhere, he attempts to steer between the opposite heresies of Pelagianism and Manichaeism. His greatest contribution is unquestionably his powerful reinterpretation of original sin in terms of social solidarity. Sin is not merely an individual offence: it is a potent collective force, in each the work of all and in all the work of each. It is the corporate act and the corporate guilt of the entire human race, and we are bound to represent it not simply as a defect, but as a disease. Schleiermacher's design, of course, is to present an understanding of the malady that will correspond with the cure. Indeed, he makes it clear that at every point the doctrine of sin is a proleptic inference from the doctrine of redemption.

The presentation of Christ's person and work, like everything else in part two of *The Christian Faith*, follows in detail the rubrics of the orthodox dogmatics. But Schleiermacher does not merely reaffirm the old doctrines, and it is not difficult to identify the two controlling thoughts in his proposals for revision. In the first place, Christ is the Redeemer because in him, and him alone, the possibility given to human nature by original perfection was realized. He stands apart from us all as the Second Adam, who lived a life of sinless perfection, a life of unbroken communion with God in total commitment to God's kingdom. This, of course, is an assertion of faith, though Schleiermacher tried in his lectures on the life of Jesus to show its compatibility with the historical sources. And in the dogmatic work he makes the idea of Jesus' perfect God-consciousness the bridge to the orthodox dogma that in Christ we have both true man and true God. For the constant potency of Jesus' consciousness of God must have been nothing less than an actual being of God in him, from which proceeded all his activity. Jesus can redeem us because he needed no redemption for himself, and we are conscious that whatever fellowship we have with God is imparted to us by the Redeemer—which is what we mean by 'grace'.

In the second place, Christ is the Redeemer by bringing into existence a new corporate life that works against the corporate life of sin. His work, to be sure, is the communication of his sinless perfection: he assumes believers into the power of his unique consciousness of God. He does this, however, neither by the kind of immediate encounter that was possible during his earthly ministry, nor merely by his teaching and example, but precisely through the new corporate life that he brought into being. It is not Christ's sufferings and death that redeem us: his passion was the consequence of his redemptive activity in establishing the new corporate life. The objectivity of the Atonement, for Schleiermacher, lies in the fact that with Christ something entirely new entered human history and created a new humanity and a new world, not just new persons. Although not everyone can be drawn all at once into the sphere of the new corporate life, we can only say of those who are passed over that they are *not yet* regenerated. The distinction between the elect and the non-elect rests solely on God's good pleasure (Calvin was right about that), but it is a vanishing distinction because there is only one eternal decree, not two, and it embraces all humanity in Christ.

The move from an individual to a corporate perspective on sin and grace makes Schleiermacher pre-eminently a theologian of the church, in which, as he puts it, the redemptive forces of the Incarnation are implanted. (In the 'common' Spirit of the church he acknowledges a second union of the divine essence with human nature and asserts that it is the function of the doctrine of the Trinity, as the keystone and not the foundation of dogmatics, to affirm and protect this twofold union.) A similar move from part to whole characterizes his discussion of creation and preservation in part one of *The Christian Faith*, which deals with the more general religious consciousness presupposed by, and contained in, the distinctively Christian religious affections. Here, too, Schleiermacher's dogmatic method enables him to set aside the difficulties posed by the opening chapters of Genesis. He did not assign canonical authority to the Old Testament anyway; but he contends that even if the narrative of the creation were accepted as revealed information about the way the world began, it would have no pertinence to the analysis of the present-day Christian consciousness. The doctrine of creation simply develops the theme of the 'feeling of absolute dependence', which Schleiermacher now (in the introduction to *The Christian Faith*) identifies as the abstract essence of the religious consciousness in every religion.

Everything positive in the doctrine of creation can be subsumed under divine preservation, of which we are conscious as the feeling of absolute dependence is combined with our perception of the world around us. And the word 'preservation' lends itself to Schleiermacher's characteristic desire always to adopt the perspective of the whole. He does not want the concept of divine activity to be construed on the model of special providences (as we say), by which God performs individual acts of intervention in the course of nature or history. Preservation denotes God's sustaining a total law-governed system that provides an absolutely reliable stage for the Incarnation and redemption. Not only is there no need for the apparent conflict of religion and science that arises when the doctrine of creation is taken from the book of Genesis; in actual fact, the interests of piety and the interests of natural science coincide, since both presuppose a concept of nature as a seamless nexus of orderly events. But only through the experience of redemption by Christ, explicated in part two, do we understand that the absolute causality of part one is the God of love, and that by creation everything is disposed with a view to the revelation of God in the flesh and the formation of the kingdom of God. Love is the foundation on which everything else in our consciousness of God is built up.

Schleiermacher did not found a school, but his thoughts on dogmatic method and his reinterpretations of old dogmas have exercised an enduring influence on Christian thought in the modern period. Some of his ideas have passed (often unacknowledged) into the mainstream of

Protestant theology; others have been kept alive partly by continuous criticism. Unfortunately, the criticism is still hindered, as it was in Schleiermacher's day, by misunderstandings, or at least by failure to examine closely his own programmatic statements on what he was doing. Despite his express warnings, the progression of topics in *The Christian Faith* has been read as the unfolding of a linear argument, or of the experiential steps on the way to becoming a Christian. He did not in fact see himself advancing from foundations (in the Introduction), through a developed natural theology (part 1), to revealed Christian theology (part 2); neither did he picture anyone first having a feeling of absolute dependence, then acquiring a general theistic belief, and finally ascending to faith in Christ. Had he wished, he said, he could have reversed the order of the two parts of his system, and he insisted that the introduction strictly lay outside dogmatics proper. The feeling of absolute dependence and the consciousness of God as creator and preserver are abstractions from the Christian faith, whose distinctive affirmations are to be explicated in the main part of the work—whether it comes first or second. The introduction is not part of the explication: it serves only to define its distinctive object and to specify the method to be used. No foundation can be established for the Christian way of believing—unless we wish to say that the explication is itself the foundation.

Blackwell, Albert L., *Schleiermacher's Early Philosophy of Life: Determinism, Freedom, and Phantasy* (1982).

Clements, Keith (ed.), *Friedrich Schleiermacher: Pioneer of Modern Theology* (1987).

DeVries, Dawn, *Jesus Christ in the Preaching of Calvin and Schleiermacher* (1996).

Duke, James O., and Streetman, Robert F. (eds.), *Barth and Schleiermacher: Beyond the Impasse?* (1988).

Forstman, Jack, *A Romantic Triangle: Schleiermacher and Early German Romanticism* (1977).

Funk, Robert W. (ed.), *Schleiermacher as Contemporary* (1970).

Gerrish, B. A., *A Prince of the Church: Schleiermacher and the Beginnings of Modern Theology* (1984).

—— *Continuing the Reformation: Essays on Modern Religious Thought* (1993).

Hinze, Bradford E., *Narrating History, Developing Doctrine: Friedrich Schleiermacher and Johann Sebastian Drey* (1993).

Johnson, William Alexander, *On Religion: A Study of Theological Method in Schleiermacher and Nygren* (1964).

Lamm, Julia A., *The Living God: Schleiermacher's Theological Appropriation of Spinoza* (1996).

Niebuhr, Richard R., *Schleiermacher on Christ and Religion: A New Introduction* (1964).

Redeker, Martin, *Schleiermacher: Life and Thought*, ET (1973).

Richardson, Ruth Drucilla (ed.), *Schleiermacher in Context* (1991).

Spiegler, Gerhard, *The Eternal Covenant: Schleiermacher's Experiment in Cultural Theology* (1967).

Thiel, John E., *God and World in Schleiermacher's* Dialektik and Glaubenslehre: *Criticism and the Method of Dogmatics* (1981).

Williams, Robert R., *Schleiermacher the Theologian: The Construction of the Doctrine of God* (1978).

Wyman, Walter E., Jr., *The Concept of* Glaubenslehre: *Ernst Troeltsch and the Theological Heritage of Schleiermacher* (1983).

XIV

Georg Wilhelm Friedrich Hegel (1770–1831)

ANDREW SHANKS

The son of a civil servant of the duchy of Württemberg, as a young man (1788–93) Hegel studied at the Lutheran theological seminary in Tübingen, where he became a close friend of two fellow students, the future philosopher Schelling and the future poet Hölderlin. Thereafter he worked as a private tutor, in Bern and Frankfurt, before joining Schelling as a lecturer at the University of Jena in 1801. His career was severely disrupted by the chaos of the Napoleonic wars. Following the battle of Jena in 1806 he lost his job, becoming first a newspaper editor and then a schoolteacher, in Nürnberg. Eventually, however, in 1816 he was appointed professor of philosophy at Heidelberg; and then in 1818 moved to the University of Berlin. Here he was a colleague of Schleiermacher's, with whom he had a rather uneasy relationship. His Berlin years brought him widespread fame and recognition.

Hegel's mature philosophy of religion has been interpreted in a bewildering variety of ways. He himself claimed that it amounted to a systematic philosophical vindication of orthodox Lutheran faith; and this was the way his 'right-wing' disciples also interpreted it. Kierkegaard's hostile polemic is a response to the flourishing of right-wing

Hegelianism in the Danish Lutheran church of the 1840s. But his portrait of Hegel as a straightforward apologist for 'Christendom'— simply seeking, by philosophical means, to render faith easier for the liberal bourgeoisie—is nevertheless quite clearly a grotesque caricature.

Others of Hegel's immediate admirers, on the other hand (the 'left-wingers') have tended to regard his profession of religious orthodoxy as a regrettable veneer, overlying the deeper critical truth of his teaching. The most notable nineteenth-century representatives of this attitude included such thinkers as D. F. Strauss, Feuerbach, and Marx. Some have even gone so far as to suggest that Hegel himself was really a covert atheist. Certainly, one may well question just how orthodox a Lutheran he was: in terms of theological heritage, he is actually perhaps more a follower of the mystic Jacob Boehme than of Luther. Already in his lifetime he was being accused, by more conservative theologians, of being a pantheist, a charge to which he responded with scorn, questioning whether the term 'pantheism' ever has any real value in philosophical discussion. His own formula for the relationship of his philosophy to Christian religion is that it shares an identical content, but in another form. Arguably, however, Hegel is in fact not only the most radically philosophical of Christian thinkers, but also the most profoundly Christian of philosophers, who developed a distinctive christology.

Thanks to the survival of a number of early manuscripts, dating from the period 1793–1800 and unpublished in his own day, we are able to trace the original gestation process of Hegel's thought. These early writings are not yet the work of a philosopher; rather, Hegel writes here as a would-be religious reformer. Indeed, they constitute a savage indictment of church Christianity in general, resting on two main objections. In the first place, he urges the desirability of a true folk religion. This would be the self-expression of a politically free-spirited people, by means of a richly celebratory representation of their *own* culture and history. At this stage, he sees the paganism of ancient Greece as an ideal model of folk religiousness. And bible-bound contemporary Christianity suffers badly from the contrast, in that its sacred narratives derive from a world that is alien to that of the actual worshippers.

Then, secondly, he has an Enlightenment rationalist line of argument. He invokes the authority of Jesus against the church. In his writings of 1795–6 especially, he portrays Jesus essentially as a teacher of pure Kantian ethics. Later, in *The Spirit of Christianity and Its Fate* (1798–9), he turns against Kant, because of the lack of an adequate 'folk-religious' element in Kantian theology. But throughout these early writings Hegel's basic diagnosis remains the same: the tragedy of Christianity is that the world of Jesus' day was not yet ready for the purity of his teaching. In *The Spirit of Christianity* we are told that what Jesus established was a community grounded in pure love, alone; but that that could not be sustained; and so the doctrine of Incarnation emerged, simply in order to provide another, more effective basis for church unity, albeit at the cost of a complete sacrifice of rationality. It is only after Hegel became a philosopher, in his Jena years, that he came to see that the Incarnation might, after all, have another meaning.

Yet there is a sense in which his whole philosophy then takes shape, fundamentally, as an elaborate strategy for explicating that other meaning. The first formulation of Hegel's mature christology comes right at the end of his Jena text, *Faith and Knowledge* (1802), where he defines the very essence of philosophic truth as a 'speculative Good Friday'. This is further associated with a description of his own age as one which is, as never before, haunted by the feeling that 'God is dead'.

The main argument of *Faith and Knowledge* is a critique of three philosophical responses to this crisis—what might be called theological agnosticism in its Kantian and Fichtean forms, and what might be called the fideism of Jacobi, also associated with Schleiermacher— all of which, in Hegel's view, fail because of a lack of adequate historical self-awareness. But for the post-Enlightenment 'death of God' to be transformed into a 'speculative Good Friday' requires the truth of theological tradition to be resurrected in quite another mode of philosophy: one which would, by contrast, be absolutely exposed to all the vicissitudes of history, inasmuch as it defines the wisdom at which it aims precisely as the most deeply considered, and most comprehensively articulated, registering and reconciliation of all the various opposing spiritual pulls of the age. Such absolute exposure, or vulnerability, of thinking to historical experience is just what Hegel henceforth terms 'absolute knowing'. 'Speculative' becomes his technical term for a thinking which refuses to rest content with the sort of hard-and-fast distinctions giving fixed answers to questions whose real significance shifts, depending on context. He completely repudiates any other foundation for metaphysics. And this is also the basic sense in which he thinks philosophy will always need religion: since it is, above all, at the level of religious experience that the shocks are first felt, which philosophy then has to deal with.

The dogma of the Incarnation thus becomes in the first instance, for Hegel, a metaphor for the necessary self-emptying of true speculative thought; its systematic abandonment of any defence mechanisms, against even the most immediately traumatic of new insights. Hence, too, his revival of the doctrine of the Trinity. The whole structure of his explicit discussion of Christian theology is Trinitarian: in the *Phenomenology of Spirit* (1807), in the *Lectures on the Philosophy of Religion* (1821–31), and again in Part 3 of the *Encyclopaedia of the Philosophical Sciences* (1830). Hegel's Trinitarianism is a direct development of his commitment to the idea of a 'speculative Good Friday'.

Already in the earliest patristic versions of Trinitarian doctrine, God the Father is not only the God of Israel to whom Jesus prayed but also, for the most part implicitly, the God of Platonist philosophy, set over against the Son and the Holy Spirit somewhat as the pure conceptual thinking of philosophy—oriented towards the eternal and unchanging universal first principles of thought—is set over against the particular stories and images of popular faith. (In this respect the roots of the doctrine are actually in the pre-Christian Jewish Platonism of Philo.) Even though he does not himself discuss the early historical emergence of the doctrine as such, Hegel for the first time renders that implicit dynamism fully explicit.

For him, the life of the Trinity consists of the dialectical interrelationship between three modes of thought. In the 1831 *Lectures on the Philosophy of Religion* he expresses this in terms of three kingdoms. The 'immanent Trinity' is not just posited as existing, unthinkably, prior to the revelation of the 'economic Trinity' in salvation history. Instead, it appears as the specific truth of 'the kingdom of the Father', the domain of pure philosophic universality. Salvation history, for him, simply *is* the interplay between pure philosophy—the first kingdom— and that which is religiously other to it, in the other two. This otherness is, on the one hand, the truth of 'the kingdom of the Son': a thinking that is, as it were, incarnate in the passions of religious experience, as codified by theological dogma. And on the other hand it is the truth of 'the kingdom of the Spirit', emerging in and through the practical life of the community of faith, as that community has interacted with its environment, and so also with the challenge of pure philosophy.

The point is that to think about God is to think about authentic thinking; and vice versa. In Christian terms, thinking at its ethically most significant is a 'speculative Good Friday'. But in order to grasp this, in its full significance, it has to be thought through in all three of these modes. First, the fixed formulaic answers of un-'speculative' metaphysics have to be dissolved. Secondly, an appropriate language must be found, for thoughtful religious faith. Thirdly, against that twofold background, it is necessary for the thinking of each generation to orient itself as clearly as possible to its own distinctive historical situation.

Three modes of thought, three tasks. Hegel pursues the first task, systematically, in his *Science of Logic* (1812–16) and in the first two parts of the *Encyclopaedia*, on logic and philosophy of nature. The third task is really the dominant concern underlying his various Berlin lecture series—on the philosophy of history, the history of philosophy, aesthetics, and religion—and his *Philosophy of Right* (1821). His handling of the second, more specifically christological, task is less clearly demarcated in textual terms than the other two.

Nevertheless, it remains pivotal. The key text in this regard is the *Phenomenology of Spirit*. At first sight the christological elements here may seem peripheral; yet appearances are deceptive. For, right at the heart of his argument in this work, Hegel moves on beyond the notion of the 'speculative Good Friday' to another, supplementary, level of christological interpretation. In effect, he sets out to answer the question first rigorously posed, and answered, by Anselm: *Cur deus homo?* Why a God-man; what exactly is it about the human condition that required God to become incarnate, as the necessary means of our salvation? Hegel does not directly discuss the Anselmian doctrine, as such. But his is arguably the classic alternative answer to Anselm's.

The *Phenomenology* is an extraordinarily difficult work, seeking as it does to explore the processes of *Geist* (spirit/mind, both human and divine) at every level of experience, from the simplest and most private to the most complex of cultural constructs. But, throughout, the basic issue remains the same. *Geist* is the drive towards open-mindedness. What Hegel presents is a linked series of portraits, depicting various types of mentality, each one in terms of the limitations it tends to impose upon one's actually learning from one's own experience. One of the most fundamental requirements of *Geist*, however, is clearly the sheer elementary self-confidence to trust one's own experience, even when it conflicts with culturally reinforced prejudice. Hegel's term for this is 'freedom of self-consciousness'. And his name for the mental servitude it overcomes is 'unhappy consciousness'.

Unhappy consciousness may be either religious or irreligious in form, but it appears at its clearest where the false inner censor-self projects itself in the image of a despotic Lord God. Hence its clearest overcoming would be in a theology that decisively did away with that image. It is not enough for freedom of self-consciousness to be expressed in a merely abstract philosophizing, like that of Stoicism; nor is it enough for it to take shape as a merely playful all-encompassing scepticism. It needs religious embodiment. And that is why it is necessary for the Lord God to become kenotically incarnate in a human individual; in the Pauline formula, 'taking the form of a servant'.

Thus, the truth of the Incarnation is a universal truth about human individuality in general: 'the infinite value of the individual as such.' But the problem is that by its very nature religious symbolism particularizes, and the universal truth is all too easily concealed behind the particularity of the representative Individual. So it becomes the essential vocation of Christian philosophy to point beyond that particularity to the universal truth it represents. For Anselm, by contrast, the necessity of the Incarnation lies in the absolute difference of Christ from all other mortals: only his sufferings, as suffered by God, are infinite, and therefore adequate by way of compensation for the strictly infinite gravity of human sinfulness as an offence against God. But Hegel's educational, rather than juridical, soteriology has diametrically opposite implications.

There is no direct reference in the original passage on unhappy consciousness either to God or to Christ. This reticence is imposed by the sheer universality of the phenomenon. Yet the whole discussion is filled with more or less veiled allusions to Christian history, since that is where the issue most directly comes to a head. And then in the penultimate chapter of the *Phenomenology* unhappy consciousness reappears, this time explicitly associated with late Roman paganism, in its 'death-of-God' despair, preparing the way for Christian faith.

In his overall philosophy of history, Hegel sets out to construct a fully comprehensive account of the emergence of freedom of self-consciousness to full articulacy. The Incarnation forms the 'speculative mid-point' of this larger story, which moves from the beginnings of civilization right up to its culmination in the historical context that had, at long last, rendered possible Hegel's own clarification of the gospel. Of each form of civilization, Hegel's underlying question is: to what extent has it provided a truly effective cultural framework for the corporate affirmation of such freedom? Here, the religious-reforming impulse of his earliest essays resurfaces, transmuted into philosophical form. Ultimately, he now argues, the ideal context for freedom is a Christian culture organized in the form of a liberal secular state; with a strongly rooted religiousness, purged of unthinking traditionalism by the cumulative shocks of the Reformation, the Enlightenment, and the French Revolution.

On the basis of subsequent historical experience, one may well question the durability of this actual conclusion. But the abiding challenge of Hegel's thought surely lies not so much in his historically limited conclusions as in his formulation of the basic criteria for theological truth, and in the way he thereby systematically opens the tradition up to creative further development.

Hegel, G. W. F., *Faith and Knowledge* (1802), ET (1977).

—— *Phenomenology of Spirit* (1807), ET (1977).

—— *Early Theological Writings*, ed. T. M. Knox (1948).

—— *Lectures on the Philosophy of Religion*, ed. Walter Jaeschke (1983–5), ET (1984–7).

Fackenheim, E., *The Religious Dimension in Hegel's Thought* (1967).

Houlgate, S., *Freedom, Truth and History: An Introduction to Hegel's Philosophy* (1991).

Jaeschke, W., *Reason in Religion: The Formation of Hegel's Philosophy of Religion* (1990).

Küng, H., *The Incarnation of God* (1987).

Lauer, Q., *Hegel's Concept of God* (1982).

O'Regan, C., *The Heterodox Hegel* (1994).

Shanks, A., *Hegel's Political Theology* (1991).

Toews, J., *Hegelianism: The Path Towards Dialectical Materialism, 1805–1841* (1980).

Walker, J., *History, Spirit and Experience* (1995).

Williamson, R. K., *Introduction to Hegel's Philosophy of Religion* (1984).

Yerkes, J., *The Christology of Hegel* (1983).

XV

John Henry Newman

(1801–1890)

ADRIAN HASTINGS

Newman was the most powerful theological mind writing in English in the 19th century and the most creative and influential Catholic thinker of his time. Among theologians he was exceptional as a master of language, excelling not only in clarity and the precise formulation of an argument but also, more unexpectedly, in irony, in an up-to-date, almost racy, debating style, as well as in the use of metaphor and poetic form. Beginning his career as a Calvinist evangelical, he ended it as a Roman cardinal. Entering the Catholic Church in England when it was still a tiny, much-hated minority within a Protestant nation, he transformed their relationship by his long-term influence upon both sides so that, in retrospect, he can be seen as the supreme reconciler.

Newman was born into a middle-class London family. He entered Oxford University when only 16 and in 1822 was elected a fellow of Oriel College. Here he became one of a remarkable group, including John Keble, Edward Pusey, and Hurrell Froude, young men intent on raising educational and moral standards in the university as well as revivifying the Church of England, which they saw as threatened both by traditional lassitude and by the inroads of liberalism. Newman emerged as the outstanding intellectual leader of this group but no less as a spiritual teacher who, in 1828, was appointed vicar of the University Church of St Mary where his sermons, regularly published, exerted a national influence.

Little by little Newman cut himself free of his early evangelicalism but not, for many years, of a deep distrust of Rome, which he saw as a profoundly corrupt church. Fascinated by the early fathers, he set himself to map out and defend an Anglican *via media* between Protestantism and Rome, a doctrinal, sacramental, and episcopal position grounded in patristic scholarship and defensible against Erastian belittlement of the church's freedom and liberal attacks on its traditional doctrines. Such was the programme of the Tractarian or Oxford Movement, which did indeed begin to alter the ethos of Anglicanism but raised intense alarm, especially among the bishops, the more it undermined 'Protestant' and exalted 'Catholic' positions.

'Oxford will want hot-headed men, and such I mean to be, and I am in my place,' wrote Newman in 1831. His first book, *The Arians of the Fourth Century*, appeared the next year. Over the next twelve years it was followed by a massive and creative theological output. *The Prophetic Office of the Church* was published in 1837, the *Lectures on Justification* in 1838, *Tract 90* (defending the compatibility of the Thirty-Nine Articles with the decrees of the Council of Trent) in 1841, and the final major piece in the series, *The Essay on the Development of Christian Doctrine*, in 1845. In the same years no fewer than ten volumes of sermons were published, together with numerous other tracts, articles, letters, and translations. In these years Newman was essentially the university theologian, stimulated by Oxford, a master of both scholarship and controversy.

His position kept changing. The more he devised a comprehensive framework to defend the Church of England, the more he encountered two, both eventually irresolvable, problems. The first was that the leaders of his church did not recognize it. This was particularly striking and painful in the response to *Tract 90*. How can you convincingly defend a church in terms that its own leadership emphatically repudiates? The second was still more fatal. Newman came to lose confidence in the *via media* himself. The more he reflected on the patristic evidence, the more it suggested to him not a basic 'primitive' core from which both Rome and Protestantism had deviated and to which one could confidently return, but a ceaselessly developing body of doctrine with which modern Catholicism seemed all in all more validly in line than anyone else. It was essentially the conclusion of a historian. Eventually, after a long period of retreat and silence at the village of Littlemore just outside Oxford, he entered the Roman Catholic communion on 9 October 1845.

As a convert who was already a famous name, Newman found his position within Catholicism extremely difficult from the start. He had very few Catholic contacts. Rome was not a world he knew or understood though he quickly developed a deep devotion to Philip Neri, who reminded him of Keble and whose 16th-century model of an 'Oratory', a community of secular priests, he determined to follow. Intellectually his stay in Rome (1846–7) horrified him: there was no serious grappling with modern issues. Its university professors, he realized, were unthinking conservatives: 'There was a deep suspicion of change, with a perfect incapacity to create anything positive for the wants of the times.' That would remain true throughout his life. Intellectually Catholicism was in a bad way, reacting against the Reformation, the Enlightenment, and 19th-century scholarship alike with an arid scholasticism, uninterested in the serious study of either patristics or Aquinas and intensely suspicious of anyone who seemed open to one or another strand of 'liberalism'. While Newman throughout his life depicted himself as an anti-liberal, his greatness in reality derived from a growing refusal to be dominated by a 'suspicion of change'. A historian's conviction about the validity of development had made him a Catholic, but it equally brought him under Catholic suspicion, challenging as it did the profound ahistoricism of ultramontanism.

After Catholic ordination in May 1847 and a brief Oratorian novitiate he returned to England to found the Oratory in Birmingham where he remained, apart from a few months as rector of the Catholic University in Dublin, for the rest of his life. He lived to be a very old man and was still publishing well into his eighties. His essay 'On the Inspiration of Scripture' appeared in 1884. What is striking, however, is how little he published in the forty years after his conversion when compared with the production of the previous twelve years. These forty years produced only three major books: *The Idea of a University* (1852), the *Apologia pro Vita Sua* (1864), and *A Grammar of Assent* (1870). These may be supplemented by four lesser, but not unimportant publications: the article 'On Consulting the Faithful in Matters of Doctrine', which appeared in the *Rambler* (1859), the *Letter to Pusey* (mostly devoted to Marian theology and devotion) of 1864, the *Letter to the Duke of Norfolk*, replying to Gladstone in regard to Vatican I (1874), and the article on the inspiration of scripture. Each of these seven works remains significant; nevertheless their quantity is sadly limited and their subjects in several cases are somewhat marginal to theology. It is fully understandable that in his earlier years as a Catholic Newman should have held back from writing anything explicitly theological. Yet it is impossible not to ask how it happened that such an outstanding thinker contributed so little over so many years once he had become a Catholic. In particular, the paucity of sermons from his Catholic years remains perplexing.

The answer can only be that circumstances were intensely unfavourable to his work and remained so until he was too old to profit by the change. As a Catholic he had no allies of any weight, only a few disciples. While English Catholics, lay people and priests, were increasingly proud of him, their own, albeit limited, intellectual tradition was being submerged by a wave of converts who, unlike Newman, mostly adopted in a quite extreme form the beliefs, devotions, and political attitudes of Continental ultramontanism. While Newman, for instance, quietly realized that the continued temporal power of the pope over the papal states was anachronistic, damaged the church, and could happily be ended, this was regarded by ultramontanes as an attitude of betrayal. English Catholicism came to be dominated by Manning, a convert of 1851, who had for a time been influenced by Newman but who became an intense papalist and one of the principal architects of the infallibility definition of Vatican I, though he had wanted a far less limited definition than was made. But Manning was also, as Newman was not, an ecclesiastical politician of genius and for twenty-seven years the near all-powerful archbishop of Westminster (1865–92). 'I see much danger of an English Catholicism of which Newman is the highest type,' Manning wrote at the time of his appointment to Westminster. 'It is the old Anglican, patristic, literary, Oxford tone transplanted into the church. It takes the line of deprecating exaggerations, foreign devotions, ultramontanism, anti-national sympathies. In a word, it is worldly Catholicism.'

It would be hard to think of anyone much less worldly than Newman. Manning prevented him from opening a house at Oxford to provide support for Catholic students. While Newman was, briefly, rector of the new Catholic University of Dublin in the 1850s, the organizational responsibilities and strains with the Irish hierarchy were too great for someone who had anyway declined to give up his position at the Birmingham Oratory. So there he remained, cut off from any sort of university life, regular theological teaching, or ecclesiastical influence, and continually under suspicion in regard to almost anything he wrote, a suspicion fomented in Rome almost entirely by English converts. As he wrote in his journal in October 1867, 'They have too deeply impressed the minds of authorities at Rome against me, to let the truth about me have fair play while I live . . . As Almighty God in 1864 cleared up my conduct in the sight of Protestants at the end of twenty years (through the *Apologia*), so as regards my Catholic course, at length, after I am gone hence, *Deus viderit*!' In fact Leo XIII made

Newman a cardinal in 1879, as quite deliberately his first creation. 'My Cardinal,' declared Leo proudly. 'It was not easy . . . they said he was too liberal.' As Newman himself remarked, explaining why he could not refuse, 'for 20 or 30 years ignorant or hot-headed Catholics had said almost that I was a heretic'. Leo's amazing gesture altered that and yet the charge continued to be insinuated long after Newman died. His criticisms of what happened at Vatican I, his insistence on the importance of the laity, the primacy of conscience, the acceptability of evolution, and much else were all far out of line with the dominant attitudes of Victorian clerical Catholicism. But his position on development was far more than that. In principle it involved a revolution in the whole Catholic line of defending the church's position as something unchanging. A hundred years later the line had altered and Newman could be hailed as the father of Vatican II, just as he was unquestionably the principal father of modern Anglican Catholicism. If there is, inevitably, a simplistic element in such assertions, there is also much truth, although one must sadly acknowledge that if he had been treated differently in the second half of his life he would have given far more. The kind of reconciliation suggested by Vatican II between the Catholic and Protestant traditions had already been realized existentially in the life of the Victorian Catholic who never really forfeited the admiration and affections of the Anglicans he left with so heavy a heart, but for whom it was always true in his own words that 'to remain the same' it is necessary to change: 'to live is to change, and to be perfect is to have changed often.'

Newman, J. H., 'On Consulting the Faithful in Matters of Doctrine', ed. John Coulson (1961).
—— *On the Inspiration of Scripture*, ed. J. D. Holmes and R. D. Murray (1967).
—— *The Idea of a University*, ed. I. Ker (1976).
—— *Apologia pro Vita Sua*, ed. Martin J. Svaglic (1967).
—— *A Grammar of Assent*, ed. I. Ker (1985).

Brown, David (ed.), *Newman: A Man for our Time* (1990).

Cameron, J. M., *John Henry Newman* (1956).

Chadwick, Owen, *From Bossuet to Newman* (1957).

Coulson, John, and Allchin, A. M. (eds.), *The Rediscovery of Newman* (1967).

Dessain, C. S., 'What Newman Taught in Manning's Church', in *Infallibility in the Church: An Anglican–Catholic Dialogue* (1968), 59–80.

Hastings, Adrian, 'Newman as Liberal and Anti-Liberal', in *The Theology of a Protestant Catholic* (1990), 116–32.

Ker, Ian, *John Henry Newman: A Biography* (1990).

Lilly, William Samuel, *A Newman Anthology* (1875), 2nd edn. Henry Tristram (1949).

Tristram, Henry (ed.), *John Henry Newman: Autobiographical Writings* (1956).

XVI

Søren Kierkegaard (1813–1855)

Hugh S. Pyper

It has been claimed that all western philosophy consists of footnotes to Plato; it seems quite as justifiable to assert that the history of 20th-century theology and philosophy largely arises from conflicting readings or misreadings of Kierkegaard. Barth, Buber, Bultmann, Derrida, Heidegger, Levinas, Marcel, Sartre, Tillich, Wittgenstein are only a few of the diverse thinkers who acknowledge their debt to Kierkegaard, although that debt is often greater than the acknowledgement would indicate.

It is striking that the idiosyncratic works of a Scandinavian theological writer in a minority language have been so influential. These very features of his authorship, of course, increase the possibility of misreading. For most of his readers, Kierkegaard has been accessible only in translation. His virtuosic use of Danish and the poetic and literary values intrinsic to his style are obscured. Another consequence is that his carefully planned output was published piecemeal in other languages. For instance, the fact that the posthumous polemic, the *Attack upon Christendom*, was the first work of Kierkegaard's to appear in German tended to brand him for German scholars as the champion of an individualistic and headily radical Christianity. Also obscured is the context: the philosophical, theological, and social debates of Copenhagen in its Golden Age, to which Kierkegaard was a witty, ironic, sometimes scathing, always controversial, but above all passionately engaged contributor.

Yet even for his Danish contemporaries the sheer quantity of his writing, much of it produced in an astonishing burst of creativity in the last ten years of his life, formed an obstacle to comprehending his message. In addition to twenty-five published works, his papers and journals run to some thirty thousand pages. This mass is compounded by its variety. Kierkegaard deploys a whole cast of pseudonyms. The relationships between these figures and how representative they are of his own positions have remained vexed questions. Only too often, later authors have cited quotations from the pseudonymous works as a simple statement of Kierkegaard's own views whereas he specifically pleads that they should be attributed to the pseudonyms. This highly self-reflexive view of authorship, with its roots in German Romanticism, extends also to the writings under his own name which are shot through with humour and irony, often missed by earnest commentators.

All this matters the more because at the heart of Kierkegaard's authorship is a concern with the process of communication itself. If we are to believe his own account in the posthumously published *Point of View of my Work as an Author*, his whole literary production was designed from the beginning as an exercise in communicating the Christian message to those who are hardest to reach: those nominal Christians who make free with the words of the gospel without taking on board the radical challenge of its claims to the whole basis of their existence. How was the full force of its impact to be recovered? For all his philosophical and literary interests, Kierkegaard was at heart a preacher, or better still, in the true sense of the word an evangelist, although he always insisted that he wrote as one 'without authority'.

His work is often at its most original where he turns to a particular problematic biblical text and teases out its implications.

In wrestling with these issues, Kierkegaard's prime resource was his own experience. Hence, it is hardly surprising that many students of his work regard his writings as a treasure trove of psychological insights into the man and reduce his most startling insights to particular comments on his own circumstances. So much writing on Kierkegaard has been bedevilled by this that it is necessary briefly to review his life if only to sound this note of caution.

He was born and died in Copenhagen. Apart from a couple of brief sojourns in Berlin, his whole life was spent within the limited world of the Danish capital. Yet out of the events of a seemingly unexciting life he managed to create a vast body of writing, endlessly poring over his own melancholy. This he felt was inherited from his father and it was the reason he confided to himself for the seminal event of his existence—his deliberate adoption of a devil-may-care persona to provoke his fiancée Regina Olsen into breaking off their engagement. This distressing but hardly earth-shattering event fills countless pages of his journals and appears in many guises throughout his writings.

The other event of comparable impact was his dispute with the *Corsair*, a satirical journal. He complained that he was the only honourable man in Copenhagen not to be lampooned and then became, unsurprisingly, the target of a fierce attack that concentrated on the fact that his trouser legs were never of the same length. Again, this seems trivial, but Kierkegaard spoke of the horror of being 'trampled to death by geese'.

One can read his publications as a brilliant but pathologically obsessive reworking of his peculiar psychic reactions. It is at least as possible, however, that it was precisely the cast of his theological and philosophical genius that laid him open to these experiences. In any case, it is well to be wary of Kierkegaard in confessional mood. 'Kierkegaard', as much as any of his pseudonyms, may be the product of his literary imagination. What unifies these events, moreover, is that they revolve around the ambivalence of communication between the multiple personae which we adopt or have forced upon us, and demand reflection on the nature of the self in its relations to others and to God.

Central to Kierkegaard's work is his insistence on the absolute qualitative difference between God and the human. Any notion of a synthesis between the two which would open the way for an assimilation of the Christian life to the civil and ecclesiastical establishment is anathema to him. Such a radical difference, however, would seem to make any communication between God and the human impossible. For Kierkegaard, it is precisely that impossibility that came about in the Incarnation. Jesus is the absolute paradox of the conjunction of divine and human, the God-man. Like Anselm in *Cur deus homo*, Kierkegaard bases his christology on the fact that only such a figure could allow for communication between God and humanity.

In this refusal to soften the paradox, Kierkegaard is standing out against the prevailing Hegelianism of the young Danish intellectuals of his day. Hegel's central theological insight was to see the reconciliation of the difference between God and man in the synthesis that Jesus represented. For Hegel, God is free because he is able to manifest the qualities intrinsic to his nature; Kierkegaard's God is free because he has infinite possibility. *The Sickness unto Death* makes explicit a further implication: 'since everything is possible for God, then God is this—that everything is possible.'

Paradoxically, it is the *impossibility* of Jesus as the God-man that Kierkegaard sees as constituting his salvific role. As the concrete instance of the impossible actualized, he bursts the bonds of the necessity that masquerades as possibility in the Hegelian account. As Kierkegaard remarks in *Judge for Yourselves!*, considered as mere possibility, Christianity seems easy, attracting the plaudits of the crowd. What an illusion, however, if someone imagines that by instantiating this possibility he would draw even greater acclaim. The gospels show that the presence of God in Jesus did not lead to universal recognition of his power, but on the contrary to scandal and offence, culminating in charges of blasphemy and the crucifixion.

This means that Kierkegaard denies that there is any effect of time on this response. The eyewitness to Jesus' earthly life or the 19th-century theologian with the benefit of nearly two thousand years of reflection are alike in the difficulty they face in comprehending the scandalous fact of God become man. The much-quoted phrase from the *Concluding Unscientific Postscript* that 'truth is subjective' comes into play here. In context, this does not mean that it is up to each individual to determine truth with no regard to evidence, as if to say, 'Jesus is God if I choose to believe he is'. Kierkegaard is not a simple relativist. It is rather that even given the evidence, human beings can manifestly stand in front of the objectively presented crucified Jesus and still refuse to acknowledge the consequences for themselves of what is happening before their very eyes.

The common error is to suppose that the Kierkegaardian subject has some form of true existence prior to the fact of God's coming in Christ and is thus capable of making some objective decision. One is only a subject because one has acknowledged that coming. Truth is subjective because truth constitutes the subject. This differs crucially from the existentialist misapprehension that it is choice itself that constitutes the subject.

For Kierkegaard, the self is a process that is incomplete without the relationship to God. 'Man is not yet a self,' he declares. His insistence on the necessity of becoming an individual, which can be read as carrying a tone of Nietzschian defiance, is actually a call for the surrender of the self in any narrowly egotistic sense. Nor is it in the end a call to repudiate society and human relationships, although sometimes he seems close to advocating this. It is only as an individual in this sense that one can hope to enter into meaningful relationships. What Kierkegaard attacks is the illusion of sociability that he calls the 'mass'.

Only by extracting oneself from the mass can one begin to build a truly human social life.

The failure to become a self brings on despair, prompted by the feeling of *Angst*, translated 'dread' or 'anxiety'. Two of his most profound psychological studies, *The Concept of Dread* and *The Sickness unto Death*, explore the relationship between angst, sin, and despair in a dizzying virtuosity of insight. Fundamentally, however, these also relate to the ideas of possibility and necessity. Angst arises out of the awareness of the possibility of choice. Even before they sinned, Adam and Eve felt angst, because the existence of the forbidden created a possibility that they could not grasp. But both possibility and necessity carry the potential to reduce the existing individual to despair because both seem to reduce the scope for meaningful choice. Too much possibility leads to anxious indecision, too much necessity to anxious fatalism. The only cure for such despair is the much-quoted 'leap of faith' (an expression not often used by Kierkegaard) whereby trust in the infinite possibility of God reorients and indeed brings about authentic existence.

Once again it is maintaining the right relationship between possibility, necessity, and actuality that is the key to much of Kierkegaard's thought. His account of the development of the individual is a case in point. Commentators often lift this as a system straight from complex pseudonymous works; all our earlier caveats should be recalled. The system extracted lays out a series of stages of life: the aesthetic, the ethical, and the religious, the latter sometimes subdivided into 'religiousness A', a general religiousness and 'religiousness B', the seizing of the paradox of Christianity. These relate once again to the notions of the possible and the actual. The aesthetic stage is one in which the world seems all possibility, all play, because of a profound scepticism over the notion that any possibility can truly become actualized. The roles and poses of the aesthetic stage are so many masks that can have no real transforming effect on the unreality of the human being. The ethical stage, however, believes in choice. Possibilities can and must be actualized, not simply by reference to the individual, but to the universal consequences of the choice. Here, however, the figure of Abraham in *Fear and Trembling* interposes, Abraham who shows his trust in God by preparing to sacrifice his son, an act that no ethical system could condone. The religious stage, however, is the one that truly lives out the claim that 'God is that all things are possible', and, in particular, that the dead can be restored to life or that, in choosing between two possibilities and renouncing one, one can gain the benefit of both possibilities.

The temptation felt by many to seek a coherent philosophical system in Kierkegaard's work is liable to lead to frustration. He himself always maintained that his role was to be an irritant and a corrective, the pinch of pepper in the stew. It is certainly possible to criticize his writings for irrationalism, for a defective doctrine of the Holy Spirit, for what may seem clear misogyny and unpalatable antisemitism, and he is the last person who would accept being excused as a child of his time. These criticisms can be debated and at times answered, but his real significance is not in his systematics so much as in the mode of communication he adopts, or, more truthfully, in his awareness of the inextricable links between these two.

Many partial readings have led to many Kierkegaards. He has been seen as the champion of an ahistorical approach to Christianity who allows later thinkers to leap the chasm between the historical Jesus and the religious experience of contemporary believers. In the face of biblical criticism and historical doubt, he provides an alternative concept of truth. It is not much of a step for others to read him as a champion of the idea that Christianity is an expression of psychological needs and constructions with no connection to objective truth. On the other hand, he has been read as the radical champion of the true absurdity of Christianity in the face of the structures of established religion: the young Barth especially was fired by the iconoclasm of his later works.

His hermeneutics have been heralded as deconstructionism *avant la lettre* yet also taken up by biblicist Protestants inspired by his reverence for the scriptures. Yet others have taken him as the 'melancholy Dane', the forerunner of the analysis of despair and alienation that so characterized 20th-century thought. He is claimed as the hero or villain, depending on one's point of view, who most clearly sounded the battle cry for the individual, either the defiant champion of true freedom or the tortured guru of the fractured and destructive solipsism so often bewailed in modern theology.

The current resurgence of interest in his work may reflect an uneasiness about the various projects of demythologization, secularism, liberalism, neo-orthodoxy, and fundamentalism that came to the fore in the 20th century. All these have been profoundly influenced by readings of Kierkegaard's work that have fallen to one side or another of the paradox that he insisted on holding in tension. As the projects of the 20th century peter out, the prospect of new shoots from that common root will form a vital resource for the Christian thinkers of the new millennium.

A complete annotated edition of Kierkegaard's works is in preparation under the editorship of H. V. and E. H. Hong (Princeton University Press).

Ferguson, H., *Melancholy and the Critique of Modernity* (1995).

Gouwens, D. J., *Kierkegaard as Religious Thinker* (1996).

Hannay, A., *Kierkegaard* (1983).

King, G. H., *Existence, Thought, Style* (1996).

Matuštík, M., and Westphal, M. (eds.), *Kierkegaard in Post/Modernity* (1995).

Pattison, G., *Kierkegaard and the Crisis of Faith* (1997).

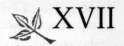

XVII

Pierre Teilhard de Chardin

(1881–1955)

URSULA KING

A French Jesuit, Teilhard was a distinguished scientist of human origins, a fervent Christian mystic, and a prolific religious writer. Throughout his life he reflected on the meaning of the Christian gospel in the light of modern science, especially in relation to evolutionary theory. Born in the volcanic Auvergne in central France into an ancient noble family, and related to Voltaire, he was deeply influenced by his natural environment. Brought up in a traditional Catholic milieu marked by a vibrant faith and strong religious practice, Teilhard was endowed with a deeply pantheistic and mystical orientation, evident from his earliest years. His mystical bent and devotional life, including veneration of the Sacred Heart of Jesus and devotion to Our Lady, were much influenced by the saintly figure of his mother, whereas his scientific interests were initially stimulated by his father, who encouraged his children to collect fossils, stones, and other specimens from nature, thus laying the foundation for Teilhard's scientific studies and career.

After an excellent classical and scientific education at a Jesuit boarding school Teilhard entered the Jesuit novitiate at the age of eighteen. He was torn between his passionate love for God and his equally passionate love for understanding the natural world. He resolved this personal crisis by recognizing that he could combine his search for spiritual perfection with that for greater knowledge and understanding. When the Jesuits were exiled from France, Teilhard continued his theological studies in the south of England, at Hastings (1902–5 and 1908–12), where he was ordained in 1911. From 1905 to 1908 he taught physics and chemistry in a Jesuit school in Cairo where he first discovered his great attraction to the desert and the east.

It was in Hastings, after reading Bergson's *Creative Evolution*, that Teilhard arrived at his understanding of the meaning of evolution for the Christian faith. Evolution made him see the world anew. All becoming is immersed in a stream of evolutionary creation where every reality is animated by a 'christic element', and the heart of God is found at the heart of the world. The living world discloses itself as an all-encompassing 'cosmic, christic, and divine milieu'. His mystical experiences were followed by scientific studies in Paris, interrupted by the outbreak of the First World War, during which he served as a stretcher-bearer. There he discovered the diversity and powerful tensions of a 'human milieu' not encountered before, an experience that laid the foundations for his future speculations about the oneness of humanity. Almost daily encounters with death gave him an extraordinary sense of urgency to leave an 'intellectual testament' to communicate his vision of the world which, with all its turmoil, struggle, and becoming, he saw as animated by and drawn up towards God. Thus he wrote a series of deeply stirring personal essays interspersed with prayers and powerful confessions of faith, published only after his death as *Writings in Time of War*. These relatively little-known essays contain the seeds for all his further writings.

After the war, he obtained a doctorate for his scientific research and was appointed to a lectureship in geology at the Institut Catholique in Paris. This gave him a platform to propound his ideas about evolution and the Christian faith, which soon led him into difficulties with the church, difficulties that never went away, but increased throughout his life. In 1923 he was glad to take up an invitation to join another Jesuit researcher on a fossil expedition to the Ordos desert in China. This year in the Far East was another decisive experience that shaped much of the rest of his life. It also led to the writing of 'The Mass on the World'. Inspired by the vision of the world at dawn transfigured by the rising sun, it expresses a mystical and sacramental offering of the entire cosmos to the energy, fire, power, and presence of the divine Spirit.

Over the following years his position in Paris grew more difficult, so that China became a place of exile where he spent the greatest part of his scientific career (1926–46), regularly interspersed with expeditions and travels in east and west. It was in China that he wrote most of his essays and also his two books, *Le Milieu Divin* (1927), and *The Phenomenon of Man* (1938–40). The latter is his best-known, but probably most difficult work, published posthumously. It immediately became a best-seller.

After the Second World War, Teilhard returned to Paris where his situation in regard to the church was still so difficult that he decided to accept a research post in the United States. Lonely and marked by suffering, he spent the last four years of his life mostly in New York, where he died on Easter Sunday 1955. He left a large corpus of writings, but, whereas his scientific papers were published during his lifetime, his religious and philosophical works were banned in his lifetime and became widely known only years later.

Life and thought are closely interwoven in Teilhard's work, which draws integrally on the experiential, emotional, and rational sides of the human being. His central method consists of a combination of outer and inner seeing, leading to a profound transformation of the world as seen, so that *seeing more* also implies *being more*. He often speaks about this 'seeing', especially in *The Phenomenon of Man*. Such seeing involves all the detailed knowledge of the outer world that science has to offer, but combined with a unifying inner vision. Teilhard's vision brought together cosmic, human, and divine dimensions, all centred in Christ and all involved in a process of becoming, or genesis. Whereas cosmogenesis refers to the birth of the cosmos, anthropogenesis and noogenesis refer to the specifically human dimension and the birth of thought. All these processes of growth are studied by modern science, whereas Christogenesis or the birth of God in Christ, as an event of cosmic significance, can only be seen through the eyes of faith. For Teilhard cosmic and human evolution are moving onwards to an ever fuller disclosure of the Spirit, culminating in 'Christ-Omega', because the divine spirit is involved in the evolutionary process at every stage.

This rise is not automatic; its outcome can never be taken for granted. It involves human responsibility and co-creativity, so that Teilhard's mind was much exercised by the moral and ethical responsibilities for shaping the future of humanity and the planet. He enquired into the spiritual resources needed to create a better quality of life and greater human integration. The heritage of the different world faiths is most important in this context. Human beings are fully responsible for their own further self-evolution, for a higher social and cultural development and a greater unification of the human community, but ultimately these goals are only achievable through the power of love. Central to his thinking were the ideas of the 'noosphere' and the 'divine milieu'. While interrelated, the first can be seen as belonging to a more secular, the second to a religious context. Given our modern scientific and technological developments, especially in information and media technology, one can see that Teilhard's idea of the noosphere (or sphere of mind) as a layer of thinking and interacting that connects people around the whole globe marks a new stage in human evolution. But the noosphere is not only a thinking layer; it is also an active sphere of love, creating greater bonds of unity between individuals and groups. The model of the noosphere provides a particularly creative perspective on racial, cultural, and religious pluralism in the new context of global complexity. Using an organic metaphor Teilhard sees Christianity, and especially the Catholic Church, as a 'phylum' channelling the unitive power of love. He was convinced that we must study the power of love in the same way that we study all other forces in the world.

Teilhard's spirituality, a unique blend of science, religion, and mysticism, was forged through much suffering and loss, yet centred on the presence of divine love disclosed through the Incarnation, creating a 'divine milieu' where God's presence shines through all things. He possessed a deep, intimate love of the human Jesus and the Christ of the cross and Resurrection. A profound panchristic mysticism was the core of his faith and the centre of his worship. As he often used the images of fire and heart, drawn from the bible and the Christian mystics, one can describe his spirituality as a fire and heart mysticism, at once modern and ancient. In its affirmation of and openness to the world as God's creation it belongs to the kataphatic rather than apophatic type of Christian mysticism. It expresses a creation spirituality 'that acknowledges love as the clearest understanding we have of God, of ourselves, of history, and the cosmos' (David Tracy).

Teilhard spoke of the 'three natures' of Christ: the human, divine, and cosmic. His reflections on the universal, cosmic Christ contain elements for a further development of christology, never presented in fully systematic form. The 'apostle of the cosmic Christ', as he once described himself, held such a dynamic, innovative, and at the same time faithful view of Christianity that he provided the outlines for a new interpretation of the Christian faith in the modern world. But traditional Christians often find his ideas challenging and unsettling. During his lifetime the Catholic Church found it difficult to accept the scientific teaching on evolution, especially regarding human origins, which contradicted the biblical stories of human creation and the Fall. It was an early paper on original sin, reinterpreted in the light of evolution, which first brought Teilhard into trouble. Several church authorities dealt rather harshly with him, but he experienced much loyal support and friendship from some members of his order, especially Henri de Lubac and René d'Ouince, his long-time superior, who described the vicissitudes of Teilhard's life as those of 'a prophet on trial' in the church of his time. He also had much support from several women friends, especially his cousin Marguerite Teillard-Chambon and Lucile Swan.

Teilhard's ideas had some influence on Vatican II and helped to shape some of its documents, especially *Gaudium et Spes*. Less hostile than before, the Catholic Church has in recent years acknowledged his contribution to Christian life and thought on several occasions. But in spite of the great interest in Teilhard's ideas during the 1960s, he has not been sufficiently valued among Christians, nor have his important ideas been adequately debated and critically evaluated in mainstream academic and intellectual life. Yet like his countryman Pascal before him, Teilhard attempted to provide an explanation of the Christian faith for the liveliest minds of his age: a modern apologetic, bringing science, religion, and mysticism together. Often his ideas are cited out of context, and the full extent of his work, most of which is out of print in English, is known and properly appreciated by relatively few. Some critics have accused him of being a New Age prophet, but this completely ignores the profoundly Christian core of his vision.

What is Teilhard's legacy for Christian thought today? He did not create a great doctrinal synthesis in the manner of traditional theologians but rather provided seminal elements for developing theological and philosophical thinking in new directions. It is his diversity and complexity which many find disconcerting. His work contains challenging reflections on God and the world, the figure of Christ, science and religion, on ecological responsibilities, interfaith encounter, the greater unification of humanity, the place of the feminine and of love in creating greater unity, and the central importance of spirituality and mysticism in religious life. His new mysticism of action is directed to both the creative transformation of the outer and inner world and the deepest communion with the living God of love, intimately present throughout creation. More than anything else it is his powerful affirmation of the Incarnation and his vision of the universal, cosmic Christ within an evolutionary perspective that reaffirm the core of the Christian faith for our scientific age.

Teilhard de Chardin, P., *The Phenomenon of Man* (1959).
—— *Le Milieu Divin* (1960).
—— *The Future of Man* (1964).
—— *Writings in Time of War* (1968).
—— *Science and Christ* (1968).
—— *Human Energy* (1969).
—— *Christianity and Evolution* (1971).
—— *The Heart of Matter* (1978).
—— *Pierre Teilhard de Chardin: Writings Selected with an Introduction by Ursula King* (1999).
Cuénot, C., *Teilhard de Chardin: A Biographical Study* (1965).
de Lubac, H., *The Religion of Teilhard de Chardin* (1967).
King, Th. M., and Wood Gilbert, M. (eds.), *The Letters of Teilhard de Chardin and Lucile Swan* (1993).
King, U., *Spirit of Fire: The Life and Vision of Teilhard de Chardin* (1996).
—— *Christ in All Things: Exploring Spirituality with Teilhard de Chardin* (1997).
Lyons, J. A., *The Cosmic Christ in Origen and Teilhard de Chardin* (1982).
Zaehner, R. C., *Evolution in Religion: A Study in Sri Aurobindo and Pierre Teilhard de Chardin* (1971).

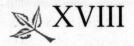

XVIII

Rudolf Bultmann (1884–1976)

James F. Kay

Bultmann was the 20th century's most influential interpreter of the New Testament, whose controversial programme of demythologizing largely set the terms for theological discussion throughout the 1950s and early 1960s.

Born into a Lutheran parsonage in Wiefelstede, Germany, Bultmann began his university studies in 1903 in the centres of the reigning Protestant liberalism, first Tübingen, then Berlin (under Hermann Gunkel and Adolf Harnack), and finally Marburg (under Adolf Jülicher, Wilhelm Herrmann, and Johannes Weiss). Encouraged by Weiss to pursue a doctorate in NT, Bultmann stayed on in Marburg, immersing himself in the comparative methods of the history of religions school typified in Wilhelm Bousset.

While teaching in Breslau in 1916, Bultmann gave the first open sign, in a letter to Martin Rade, of his break with liberal theology. His disenchantment came with the realization that the liberal 'lives' of Jesus, biographies written to inspire faith, had now been rendered untenable by scholarly research that squarely placed the gospels into the context of the myths and cult-dramas known to the Graeco-Roman world.

In 1921, Bultmann published his monumental form-critical study, *The History of the Synoptic Tradition*, still a standard today. This coincided with his return to Marburg, where he began his 30-year tenure (1921–51) as professor of NT. Here, he published his volume on the message of Jesus (1926), his theologically profound, if now historically dated, commentary on the Fourth Gospel (1941), his commentary on Second Corinthians (1976), and his four volumes of collected essays (1933–64).

Bultmann's tenure at Marburg overlapped the rise and fall of the Third Reich (1933–45). With Karl Barth and others, Bultmann was openly part of the Confessing Church, organized in 1934 in opposition to Hitler. But even as early as May of 1933, amid the full flush of Nazi enthusiasm, Bultmann had lectured to his classes that no nation is so 'pure and clean' that its will can be equated with that of God, and he called for theology to serve the nation by exercising prophetic criticism. That same fateful year, Bultmann drafted a declaration by the Marburg theological faculty opposing any extension of the new Nazi laws that would have excluded 'non-Aryans' from church office, and he vigorously defended this position in the theological press. Similarly, in 1934, he threatened to resign the editorship of a prestigious academic series if the dissertation of his Jewish student, Hans Jonas, were blocked from publication. Thus, Jonas's book on Gnosticism became one of the few by Jews published in Germany during the Nazi period. In such ways as these, Bultmann attempted a faithful Christian witness under totalitarian conditions.

Throughout his career, Bultmann consistently wedded the Kierkegaardian concept of the 'wholly other' God with the distinctive terminology of Martin Heidegger, who described human existence (or *Dasein*) as radically 'fallen' into 'inauthenticity'. Bultmann set forth his own existentialist theology and hermeneutical programme most comprehensively in his 1941 lecture 'New Testament and Mythology', which Schubert Ogden called 'perhaps the single most discussed and controversial theological writing of the century' (Ogden, p. vii).

Bultmann's retirement in 1951 was crowned by the completion of his *magnum opus*, *Theology of the New Testament*, and his visit to the United States where he gave the Shaffer Lectures at Yale, later published as *Jesus Christ and Mythology*. In 1953 he delivered the Gifford Lectures in Edinburgh on the theme of 'History and Eschatology'. By the early 1960s, which witnessed the zenith of his transatlantic influence, Bultmann was engaging in lively, at times pained, debates with former students such as Ernst Käsemann, Günther Bornkamm, Hans Conzelmann, and Gerhard Ebeling. In opposition to their Marburg mentor, these 'post-Bultmannians' all urged a renewed quest for the historical Jesus, a task Bultmann consistently argued was misguided on both historical and theological grounds.

Bultmann held that Jesus Christ matters decisively for each individual's transition from inauthentic to authentic existence. Moreover, he was convinced that believing in Jesus Christ as one's Lord and Saviour does not mean believing in the prescientific cosmology found in the NT. Christian faith is neither a leap out of modernity, nor a retreat from intellectual honesty. One does not have to profess the mythical frameworks and formulas of yesterday in order to confess Jesus Christ today. Thus, the aim of Bultmann's theology was to show how one could responsibly embrace Christian faith in a modern age whose canons of knowledge were shaped by science.

This apologetic aim shows the kinship between Bultmann's thought and that of Protestant liberalism. Indeed, Bultmann learned from his liberal teachers that the NT accounts of Jesus intertwine historical sources and traditions with mythical motifs widely found throughout the ancient Near East and the Graeco-Roman world. With this discovery, liberalism sought to unbind the historical Jesus from the constrictions of myth by eliminating them from its dogmatics and preaching. These included a number of traditional tenets such as

Jesus' virgin birth, vicarious atonement, and bodily Resurrection. No longer handicapped by these orthodox 'absurdities', liberalism was free to emphasize the incomparable personality of the historical Jesus and to join him in proclaiming a Kingdom of God progressively developing within the historical process. Faith was interpreted to mean coming under the redeeming influence of Jesus' personality as it continues to guide humankind towards the realization of God's rule in human affairs.

Bultmann believed liberalism was right to distinguish between the historical and the mythical elements in the NT, but went on to show where, with the best of intentions, it had gone wrong. The error was in its failure to recognize that the saving significance of Jesus is never understood in the NT in a historicist sense, as a fulfilment of the world's latent possibilities; rather, it understands Jesus in an eschatological sense, as one whose coming marks the final judgement, or end of the world. This is expressed in the apocalyptic language of Paul's cross–Resurrection message or kerygma (which the Synoptic Gospels narrate) and in the Gnostic-derived concepts and framework of the Fourth Gospel, which tell of the divine Logos who comes into the world 'from above'. In other words, while the Jewish prophet Jesus of Nazareth, who proclaimed the Kingdom of God, is the historical presupposition of Christianity, it is the proclaimed destiny of this Jesus as crucified and risen, or God's eschatological salvation event, that is the real source and norm of Christian faith. The proclaimer (of the Kingdom) has become the proclaimed (of the church), and Christian faith only arises from this latter proclamation. Therefore, when the liberals eliminated apocalyptic and Gnostic myth from their portrayals of Jesus, they unwittingly eliminated the eschatological essence of the Christian faith and, hence, the significance of Jesus for salvation.

The resultant problem was how the church could continue to proclaim its eschatological understanding of salvation when that understanding was expressed in mythological language. Bultmann answered by arguing for an existentialist interpretation of NT eschatology. The point was not to eliminate the Christ-myth which expressed Jesus' saving destiny, but to translate it so that it could truly be heard as a call to authentic existence. This apologetic aim led Bultmann to advocate his famous hermeneutical programme known as 'demythologizing'.

This programme assumes that the real referent of NT mythology is not the objectivized realities of which it literally speaks—heaven, hell, Satan, atoning sacrifice, reanimated corpses, or virgin births—but rather the understanding of existence that such mythological constructs symbolize. Thus, interpreters of the NT, especially preachers of the gospel, must proceed by translating outmoded cosmological categories into modern existentialist ones. For example, Paul's mythology of the cosmic powers, which the cross of Christ overcomes (1 Cor. 2: 6–8; cf. Col. 2: 13–15), is a way of speaking of one's bondage to the norms and patterns of this world, to the past, and to vain attempts to secure existence ever threatened by suffering and death. Hence, to be 'crucified with Christ' (Gal. 2: 19–20; 5: 24; 6: 14) means to accept God's judgement on our worldly dependence and to accept God's freedom to embrace the future without fear of death.

The word that judges our past and extinguishes our old life is simultaneously the word that re-creates us; it is 'the power of God unto salvation' (Rom 1: 16). Faith means entering here and now into eschatological existence, into love for our neighbours, and into the freedom of no longer being always determined by the power of death. This message or 'the word of the cross' (1 Cor. 1: 18) is thus 'the word of life' (Phil. 2: 16). The Resurrection of Jesus is not about the resuscitation of a corpse. Such mythological language, rooted in Jewish apocalyptic, is really a way of saying that when the word of the cross is proclaimed as an appeal for authentic existence, as a call for the decision of faith, it comes alive in its hearers and effects in them the very judgement and grace it proclaims. Jesus' Resurrection is simply a 1st-century way of symbolizing the performative power of the Christian message. This is why Bultmann could agree with the formulation, hurled at him in criticism, 'Jesus has risen into the kerygma'.

Since the 1970s, commentators have noted the precipitous decline in Bultmann's popularity. In some ways, the very comprehensiveness of his theological proposals, drawn from NT exegesis and theology, history of religions, hermeneutics, systematic theology, and philosophy, has been eroded by further developments in these disciplines. Many scholars now question Bultmann's historical assumptions (e.g. that a Gnostic Redeemer myth provides the Johannine conceptuality for Jesus' saving significance), his existentialist theology (e.g. that the cosmological referents in NT eschatology can be translated without remainder into existentialist concepts), and his philosophy of language (e.g. that language is primarily the expression of existential self-understanding).

Thus, Bultmann's continuing influence does not stem from a surviving school of thought bearing his name, since the synthesis he achieved has unravelled. Rather, his continuing influence is seen (1) wherever the NT is approached through historical and comparative methods involving other ancient texts and parallels known to the history of religions; (2) wherever the saving significance of Jesus Christ is identified not with historical reconstructions but with the preaching of the Christian gospel or 'word of the cross'; and, (3) wherever talk of God is understood as revealing the self-understanding of the faith (and faith communities) out of which it emerges. This hermeneutical turn in modern theology, with its concern for the 'situation' or 'context' in which theological language arises and to which it is addressed, is Bultmann's most enduring legacy in our postmodern period.

Bultmann, R., 'New Testament and Mythology: The Problem of Demythologizing the New Testament Proclamation', in S. M. Ogden (ed.), *New Testament and Mythology and Other Basic Writings* (1941), ET (1984).

—— *Theology of the New Testament* (2 vols.; 1949–51), ET (1951–5).

Bultmann, R., (cont.), *Jesus Christ and Mythology* (1958).

Fergusson, D., *Bultmann* (1992).

Kay, J. F., *Christus Praesens: A Reconsideration of Rudolf Bultmann's Christology* (1994).

Morgan, R., 'Rudolf Bultmann', in D. F. Ford (ed.), *The Modern Theologians: An Introduction to Christian Theology in the Twentieth Century* (2nd edn. 2 vols.; 1997).

XIX

Paul Johannes Tillich

(1886–1965)

Robert P. Scharlemann

A systematic theologian and philosopher of religion, Tillich was born in Starzeddel (now Starosiedle, Poland, then in Brandenburg, Germany), the son of a Lutheran pastor. He attended the university of Berlin, from which he received his Ph.D., and the University of Halle, from which he received his doctorate in theology. After passing his second theological examination at Halle, he was ordained in 1912.

During the First World War, he served as a military chaplain. These years had a profound impact on Tillich's understanding of human reality. The effect of the war's devastation, physical and spiritual, is reflected in a letter written in November 1916: 'I have become purely an eschatologist [in that] what I, along with others, am experiencing is the actual end of the world of this time.' After completing his military service in December of 1918, Tillich received his qualification for university teaching (*Habilitation*) at the University of Berlin in 1919. That year he published one of his most influential essays, 'On the Idea of a Theology of Culture' ('Über die Idee einer Theologie der Kultur'). The essay presented the principles for interpreting culture theologically that Tillich followed throughout his career and became the basis of a new field of theological study. The guideline that he used for such an interpretation was, in his formulation, that the *Gehalt* (import, or substance) of a cultural work is 'grasped in the content (*Inhalt*) by means of the form and given expression'. Expressionistic art is an example. Here, the forms of everyday reality—for example, the shapes of people or everyday objects—are distorted in such a way as to express a power, or reality, that manifests itself by the very way in which it breaks through the form *and* content of the objects. A theology of culture interprets the meaning of this shattering reality, the 'substance', or depth-content. Accordingly, an interpretation of culture always involves a reference to three elements of cultural works: the form, the content (*Inhalt*), and the substance (*Gehalt*).

In the spring of 1929, Tillich accepted a position teaching philosophy and sociology at the University of Frankfurt. There, in 1933, he published the work that was to lead to his emigration to the United States, *Die sozialistische Entscheidung* (*The Socialist Decision*). It was a cautious analysis of socialism and a critique of unrestrained capitalism, based upon the idea of *kairos* (right time)—the idea that, even politically, there are 'right' times for accomplishing certain things— and upon an analysis of German democracy as only an abstract, not yet a real, democracy. Tillich concluded that the time was ripe for a new socialism, specifically a religious socialism that could incorporate democracy. National socialism not being what he envisaged, the essay also criticized the totalitarian element in the Nazi movement, and, as a result, Tillich became one of the many educated Germans who emigrated under the threat of those years as the movement developed.

Tillich left Germany in October 1933, and in February 1934 began his long teaching career at Union Theological Seminary in New York, remaining there until his retirement in 1955. He then became University Professor at Harvard—a great distinction—and, in 1962, with similar distinction, the Nuveen Professor of Theology at the University of Chicago. His last public address, 'The Significance of the History of

Religions for the Systematic Theologian', delivered at the University of Chicago shortly before his death on 22 October 1965, reflected the direction his thought had taken towards the questions raised by the encounter of Christianity with other religions. These differed from the questions he had treated in his earlier works because they involved differences in the religious symbols themselves.

Tillich's major work is the three-volume *Systematic Theology*, in which he undertakes to interpret Christian symbols as providing answers to ontological questions. Through the 'method of correlation', he shows how the question of the meaning of being (the ontological question) is correlated with the symbol of God as its answer (the theological answer). The symbol *God* is the reality that answers the question of the meaning of being. In the five divisions of the *Systematic Theology*, Tillich provides, on the one hand, an analysis of the three basic ways in which the ontological question is asked and, on the other hand, an interpretation of religious symbols that shows how these present the reality that answers the question of the meaning of being. Simply put, the three basic questions are these: What is the meaning of being itself? What is the meaning of (human) existence? What is the meaning of life? The first question, answered by the symbol *God*, is occasioned by the finitude of human being. The second question, answered by the symbol of the Christ, is occasioned by the contradictoriness (estrangement) of human being—the fact that things are not what they should and could be. The third question, answered by the symbol of the Spirit, is occasioned by the ambiguity of actual life—its mixture of being and nonbeing, of the good and the bad, of the creative and the destructive. The symbol *God* presents the meaning of the finitude of being; the symbol *Christ* presents the meaning of the contradictoriness of existence; and the symbol *Spirit* presents the meaning of the ambiguity of actual life. The actual human situation is that of life, in which the finitude of being and the contradictoriness of existence are always ambiguously mixed. To say that 'God', 'the Christ', and 'the Spirit' are symbols means that they actually convey the reality of the answer that they represent. In other words, as a symbol, the word 'God' (or the meaning and image borne by that word) actually presents an ultimate meaning in the finitude of being in the world; as a symbol, the word, or image, or history connected with 'the Christ' conveys a real power to bear the contradictions and meaninglessness of reality without being overwhelmed by them; and the symbol of 'the Spirit' is the actual presence of an unambiguous meaning discernible through the ambiguities of life.

Through this method of correlation, Tillich intended to assign equal importance to the question of being (the main subject matter of philosophy or ontology), and to God as the symbol in which the meaning of being is present (the main subject matter of theology). The correlation between the two is formulated in the statement 'God is being-itself'. That is to say, what is present in the *symbol* God is also the reality to which the ontological *concept* of being-itself refers.

Tillich's distinctive contribution to Christian theology lies in three characteristics of his work. The first is his application of the Protestant principle of justification to the realm of theoretical thought. One who doubts the reality of God knows the truth despite that doubt, just as one who sins is justified despite the sin; the reality of God shows itself to the human mind despite the doubt, just as the goodness of God appears in human actions despite their imperfection. The second appears in his theology of culture, which is based on the conception that culture itself is capable of expressing, indirectly, the ultimate meaning intended by religious faith. Thus, in his analysis of contemporary culture Tillich showed how it expressed indirectly what religion expresses directly. The third characteristic, which is at the basis of the method of correlation used in the *Systematic Theology*, is the idea that philosophy, which asks the question of the meaning of being as such, and religion, which is based upon the reality shown in the symbol of God, cannot be reduced to each other, and cannot be derived from each other, but can be 'correlated'. What human beings seek when they ask the question of the meaning of being can be correlated with what human beings receive through the meaningfulness of religious symbols. Accordingly, Tillich's definition of faith as 'ultimate concern'—in the sense of one's being ultimately concerned about that which concerns one unconditionally—implies both the ontological question of the meaning of being and also the symbol God as the presence of being-itself, which is beyond both being and non-being.

Tillich's wide influence, especially in the United States, is attributable to the ecumenical character of his theology, to the effectiveness of his teaching, the appeal of his work to professionals as well as to the laity, and, no doubt, to his ability to relate theology to the issues of the time.

Tillich, P., *The System of Sciences according to Objects and Methods* (1923), ET (1981).

—— 'Der Protestantismus als kritisches und gestaltendes Prinzip' (1929).

—— *The Socialist Decision* (1933), ET (1977).

—— *The Protestant Era* (essays), ed. James Luther Adams (1948).

—— *Systematic Theology* (3 vols.; 1951–63).

—— *The Courage to Be* (1952).

—— *Biblical Religion and the Search for Ultimate Reality* (1955).

—— *Theology of Culture* (1959).

—— *Christianity and the Encounter of the World Religions* (1963).

—— *Main Works/Hauptwerke*, ed. Carl Heinz Ratschow *et al.*, Ger./ Eng. edn. with introductions (6 vols.; 1989–92).

Bulman, Raymond F., and **Parrella, Frederick J.** (eds.), *Paul Tillich: A New Catholic Assessment* (1994).

Kegley, Charles W. (ed.), *The Theology of Paul Tillich*, 2nd edn. (1982).

Wehr, Gerhard, *Paul Tillich zur Einführung* (1998).

Karl Barth (1886–1968)

Bruce L. McCormack

Barth was arguably the greatest theologian of the 20th century; a thinker in whose work the unresolved problems resident in the Schleiermacherian tradition in dogmatic theology were finally overcome and that tradition found its most self-consistent expression.

Barth was born in Basel, Switzerland, of pietistic parents. His father, Johann Friedrich (Fritz) Barth, became a lecturer in NT and early church history at Bern when Karl was 2. Known as a 'positive' theologian, Fritz Barth confounded conservative expectations by embracing moderately critical approaches to the investigation of scripture. He took a strong interest in social issues (the women's rights movement, for example) and was well acquainted with the concerns of the Christian Socialist movement.

On the eve of his confirmation at the age of 15, Barth made the momentous decision to become an academic theologian so that, as he said later, he might discover what the creed was all about. He began his university studies at Bern. After completing his initial battery of qualifying exams, he followed the common practice of going abroad to study. A semester in Berlin was spent listening to Adolf Harnack, Julius

Kaftan, and Hermann Gunkel. After another Bern semester, he spent the year 1907/8 in Tübingen and Marburg. Marburg meant, above all, study with the greatest dogmatic theologian of the time, Wilhelm Herrmann. It also afforded contact with the neo-Kantianism of Hermann Cohen, a Jewish philosopher whose influence on Barth would be discernible throughout his career. Following the completion of his studies, Barth served as editorial assistant to Martin Rade, whose *Die christliche Welt* was the leading 'liberal' theological journal of the day.

After serving a *Vikariat* in a German-speaking church in Geneva, in July 1911 Barth became pastor in Safenwil, a small town whose leading industry was textiles. He had already encountered poverty in Calvin's city. But at that time, he regarded social ills fatalistically, as an unfortunate necessity of nature. In Safenwil, he very quickly (and to his own astonishment) found himself siding with the socialists. Barth's sudden theological/political transformation shortly after his arrival there provoked consternation in his family and disapproval on the part of friends and mentors in Marburg. A first address to the local Workers' Union (the base organization of the Swiss Social-Democratic Party in that area) three months after his arrival was followed by a highly provocative and well-publicized address in December with the title 'Jesus Christ and the Social Movement'. In the face of mounting criticism, Barth defended himself by saying that he could no longer preach a 'neutral "gospel" '. He had to take a decisive stand on practical issues like capitalism. We see in this early episode in Barth's pastorate a level of practical engagement which would remain characteristic of his entire career. Barth's theology had to eventuate in ethics; that was a matter of internal necessity.

The outbreak of war in August 1914 and the endorsement by his beloved theological mentors in Germany of the war policies of Kaiser Wilhelm became the catalyst for a new departure in Barth's thought. Most biographers have treated this crisis in Barth's theological existence as a 'break' with liberal theology and even with 'modernity', to the extent that the two terms were regarded as synonyms. And there can be no question that Barth experienced his shift as a rupture with the past and always interpreted it as such. With hindsight, however, we have to say that the 'break' was not as complete as Barth thought. Recent studies have shown that Barth's anti-modern rhetoric often served to conceal how thoroughly modern his new theology was. And even the 'break' with so-called 'liberal' theology was never complete. With Schleiermacher and Herrmann, particularly, Barth stood in a relationship characterized by both continuities and discontinuities. His departure from the theology of his teachers is best described as a move from an experientially based theology to a theology grounded in a dialectically conceived model of revelation.

In the summer of 1916, Barth began work on what would become the most significant theological work since the publication of Schleiermacher's *Speeches*: his commentary on Paul's epistle to the Romans. The first edition was published in November 1918, as the First World War came to an end. It belongs to a body of apocalyptic/utopian literature which emerged in that year of political and cultural convulsions: Ernst Bloch's *Geist der Utopie*, Oswald Spengler's *Decline of the West*, and Franz Rosenzweig's *Stern der Erlösung*. Written in an expressionistic style, it differed from the more famous second edition primarily through its affirmation of the possibility of experienceable irruptions of the Kingdom of God in history.

When the possibility of reissuing the commentary arose in late 1920, Barth found that a number of factors had conspired in the interim to force a complete rewrite. Intellectual influences (the 'critical idealism' of Barth's brother Heinrich and Franz Overbeck's apocalyptic reading of the NT and early church history) moved Barth to a more radical eschatology that rendered connections between the Kingdom of God and this world tenuous. Hence, the second edition of *Romans* has been rightly described as a 'violent' work (Steiner 1978: p. ix); 'violent' in the sense that the judgement of God is pronounced against the world in its totality. But the anger which comes to expression in the work has to be seen against the horizon of hopefulness that governs the whole. The judgement of God is everywhere understood to be in service of God's graciousness. Grace kills only in order to make alive. And the quasi-idealistic rendering of the critical negation to which the world is subjected is relieved, here and there, by the realistic affirmation of the bodily Resurrection of Jesus from the dead as a prolepsis of a final transformation of the world.

In 1921, Barth accepted a chair in Reformed theology at Göttingen. Five semesters of preparatory teaching in historical theology and biblical exegesis eventuated in Barth's first dogmatics lectures in the summer of 1924. *The Göttingen Dogmatics* marked a decisive move forward in Barth's thinking through his appropriation of the ancient christology of the post-Chalcedonian church and his use of it to lend coherence to his claim that revelation reaches into history without becoming a predicate of history. Barth's dogmatic method—which he continued to employ in the *Church Dogmatics* with little modification— was a function of the material decisions he made at this time in the areas of revelation, christology, and Trinity.

In 1925, Barth was called to Münster as a regular professor of dogmatics and New Testament exegesis, and in 1930 he succeeded Otto Ritschl as professor of systematic theology in Bonn. The Bonn years were notable, above all, for the role played by Barth in the 'Church Struggle' against the Nazi regime. Though Barth later acknowledged he should have been more alert to dangers posed to the Jews, his public defence of the freedom of the church to proclaim the gospel made him a leader of the resistance and a natural choice to pen the Barmen Declaration in May 1934. Barth was suspended from his teaching responsibilities in November of that year for refusing to give an unqualified oath of loyalty to the *Führer*. His dismissal the following month left him free to return to his native Basel in 1935.

His return as professor of systematic theology allowed Barth to devote himself to his *magnum opus*, the *Church Dogmatics*. A work whose contents first saw the light of day as lectures to students, its situationally driven interest in current issues in both church and society is lost to sight today without considerable archaeological labour. Its freedom from complete allegiance to any one philosophical scheme has enabled the work to remain relevant to church audiences long after the philosophies of its day were rendered outdated. Barth retired from teaching in 1962.

At the heart of Barth's theology lies a single conviction. God is in eternity (in himself) the mode of his self-revelation in time. The content of revelation (its 'what') is identical with its mode (its 'how'). The significance of this conviction may be seen through a brief comparison with Schleiermacher's theology.

In his *Christian Faith*, it was Schleiermacher's intention to overcome all speculative foundations in theology by means of a strict concentration upon the Christian's pious self-consciousness (i.e. that religious consciousness wherein the 'feeling of absolute dependence' has been *modified* by the redemption accomplished in Jesus of Nazareth). Much of his doctrine of God, however, was established by means of an idealistic derivation of grounds in God for the 'feeling of absolute dependence' *considered formally* (apart from all historical, lived modifications). Given that Schleiermacher's 'feeling of absolute dependence' has no existence in reality in the absence of modifications on the level of what he called the 'sensible' self-consciousness, he ought not to have been able to treat the religious self-consciousness *at any point* without regard for the specifically Christian experience of it. Or, if he thought he was justified in treating the doctrine of God and his relationship to the world without regard to specifically Christian experience, then he could not legitimately claim (as he did) that John 1: 14 is the basic text for all dogmatics. The unresolved problem in Schleiermacher's dogmatics is the extent to which things are said of

God which reach beyond the limits established by history and, as a consequence, perpetuate the weaknesses of classical metaphysical theism. Judged from that standpoint, Schleiermacher is rightly seen as a transitional figure with only one foot in the modern world.

The significance of Barth's work lies in his ability to close the door firmly on speculation about an abstract eternal being of God 'in himself' (i.e. essentialism). For Barth, God's being is constituted by his free decision for the incarnation of the Son and the outpouring of the Spirit in time. Hence, even before these things take place, God is in himself (by way of anticipation) what he has freely determined himself to be in time. The result is that when God incarnates himself, no change is effected in the divine being. The economic Trinity therefore becomes wholly disclosive of what God truly is in and for himself. There is no state of existence in the triune life of God which lies beyond the reach of what might be known of God in and through his self-revelation in time. And this means, in turn, that the epistemological limits placed on the human knower by history are not violated in knowing a transcendent (supramundane) God. For this reason, Barth's theology does justice to the historicizing tendencies of more than a century of theology before him (even as it establishes the proper limits of those tendencies). And in overcoming the idealistic elements in Schleiermacher's approach to dogmatics, Barth also fulfilled the promise contained in the former's adumbration of a more christocentric grounding of theology.

How did Barth arrive at these conclusions? Two doctrines were materially decisive, both developmentally and in terms of internal systematic integration. The doctrine of revelation was elaborated and honed over a period of twenty-two years (1915–36). The doctrine of election then provided the divine ontology which would ground and render fully coherent his doctrine of revelation.

With respect to the doctrine of revelation, the key concept is that of the relation of indirect identity which is established in the event of revelation between the being of God and the creaturely medium through which that being is revealed. The language of 'indirect identity' refers to the idea that, in revealing himself, God makes himself to be fully and completely present *in* a creaturely reality without divinizing that creaturely reality. In the absence of such divinization, the creaturely reality which serves as a medium of God's act of self-revelation can never become directly revelatory; the divine reality lies hidden 'beneath the surface', so to speak. If the divine reality in the medium is to be recognized, it must be revealed by the Holy Spirit. Revelation is, thus, a Trinitarian event. God the Father reveals himself in the Son through the power of the Holy Spirit. This much of Barth's doctrine of revelation was largely in place in the two commentaries on Romans. What he added in *The Göttingen Dogmatics* was a christological explanation. The meaning of the Incarnation is that the eternal Son assumed a human 'nature' and lived a thoroughly and completely human life without detriment to his deity. Basic to Barth's elaboration of this claim was his rejection of the thought that the hypostatic union of the divine and human natures in one person (or subject) gave rise to a transference of divine attributes to the human nature. Thus, the concern sounded in *Romans* remained in place: no divinization of the creature in revelation! What he could not yet explain was how the living of a human life did not produce change in God on a fundamental, ontological level.

It was in Barth's mature doctrine of election that he was finally able to advance a divine ontology which would provide the realistic ground of the whole of his theology. God, he was now able to say, is a self-determining subject who freely and eternally chose to be God in a covenant of grace with the human race and to be God in no other way. In that God made this 'primal decision', he assigned to himself the being he would have from everlasting to everlasting. There was never a time when God's being was not already determined for this covenant—and that means that the idea of an undetermined, abstract mode or state of being in God above and prior to election has been completely eliminated. God *is* in eternity what he has determined himself to be in time.

With his divine ontology firmly in place, Barth could then go on (in later volumes of the *Church Dogmatics*) to construct a human ontology consonant with it. What God and the human 'are' is defined by the covenant of grace which constitutes the material content of God's primal decision (election). God is the Lord of the covenant; we humans are his covenant-partners, chosen and created for lives of free covenant fidelity before him. Jesus Christ is the one human in history in whom this true humanity is perfectly realized. Through the reconciliation achieved in his life, death, and Resurrection and our assimilation to it by the transforming power of the Holy Spirit, our humanity is brought, moment by moment, into conformity with Christ's own.

In spite of the fact that Barth disdained a positive employment of the concept of an 'analogy of being' between God and humanity after 1929, such an analogy is implied. Formally, the analogy consists in the fact that both divine being and human being are understood by Barth to be a being-in-act (i.e. both are conceived in actualistic terms). Materially, both are structured by the covenant of grace. The dissimilarity in the analogy lies in the fact that God gives himself his being whereas we receive our being from him. The similarity lies in the fact that as and when our being is brought into conformity to Christ's own, it is made to be like his in holiness. And it is in holiness, finally, that the true positive analogy between God and the human is to be found. Admittedly, this last emphasis is drastically underdeveloped in Barth's own work and collides, in some respects, with his treatment of the *imago Dei*. Still, that his work implies an analogy of being on something other than traditional Catholic terms (i.e. as a function of created faculties or a created relation) has been largely overlooked by Barth scholars.

Barth had no interest in repristinating old theological trains of thought, though he sought to interpret them generously. For that reason, traditional characterizations of his theology as neo-orthodox are misleading. What is true is that Barth showed, more than anyone else, what being orthodox under the conditions of modernity might entail. He rejected the 'metaphysical way', which was basic to all classical forms of Christian theism, without sacrificing real knowledge of God in himself. And he did so by understanding God in himself as the mirror reflection of the God disclosed in the history of Jesus of Nazareth through the outpouring of the Holy Spirit.

At every stage of his development after 1915, Karl Barth was a cultural outsider. Even when he forsook the expressionistic style of writing in his dogmatic works, his work continued to express the 'son's revolt against the father' (Peter Gay)—embodied, above all, in the person of Schleiermacher but extending to the whole of modernity. He remained, throughout his life, strongly countercultural and combative, working out a positive vision that would do justice to the critical concerns of earlier years. Of a domestication of theology by the later Barth there can be no talk. His was the single most anti-dogmatic dogmatics produced in the modern period; anti-dogmatic in the sense that his doctrine of revelation, centred as it was in the dialectical relation of God to every medium of that revelation, would not allow for domestication. Rarely has that been fully grasped and misunderstandings abound in the stock criticisms directed against Barth's theology.

From the *Romans* period on, his rejection of natural theology made him the target of vehement opposition. What is forgotten today is that Barth's rejection of natural theology is of a piece with a lengthy history of uneasiness with natural theology which, starting with Hume and Kant, included notables like Schleiermacher and Ritschl. What made Barth a special target during his lifetime was the fact that he radicalized the critique of natural theology by defining it more broadly than previously, as any theology that failed to recognize that God is in himself the mode of his self-revelation in time. Revelation *is* God himself, speaking in person. If inferences drawn from observations of nature could produce knowledge commensurable with the self-revelation of *this* God, then Barth would have had to concede the legitimacy of natural theology. But he could not convince himself that this was possible. Debates with Barth's attitude towards natural theology which do not realize that his position can only be defeated by taking on his doctrine of revelation in its entirety (including christology, election, and Trinity) will always fail to rise above the level of a superficial quibble. To suggest that his view was a function of a necessary but transcendable polemic against Nazi ideology is completely to miss the point.

Second, Barth awakens suspicions because he is able to make such definite assertions about subjects that late-19th-century theology had taught the church it could say nothing about (e.g. election). Even where Barth speaks of subjects which are *meta*-physical in the strict sense, however, the way he takes in gaining access to them is not the metaphysical way. His 'metaphysics' (understood as a region of discourse) were strictly 'anti-metaphysical' (understood as a methodology), resting on an epistemology that respected the limits of history.

Third, Barth arouses hostility today because of his 'Christocentrism'. That was not so much of a problem in his own lifetime: virtually everyone wanted to be 'Christocentric' in some form—as the classical liberal tradition demonstrates. But today, concerns for the world religions, not to mention the desire on the part of many Christian theologians to construct an independent doctrine of the Holy Spirit, make his 'Christocentrism' an affront. The 'exclusivity' of Barth's 'Christocentrism', however, is inherently inclusive in that every human is, for him, elect in Jesus Christ. We need to recognize that today's debates over approaches to the issue of 'inclusivity' reach to the very heart of what it means to be genuinely Christian in the realm of theology. On this issue, at least, Barth would have had the whole of the classical liberal tradition on his side. It is worth pondering whether today's 'liberals' have not taken a turn that amounts to a break with their own tradition, thereby stepping out of the realm of Christian theology altogether.

In the English-speaking world, Barth's impact has yet to be assimilated fully. It may well be that the period of his greatest influence lies in the future. It was, after all, the 'first postmodernity' in Germany (Roberts 1991: 170) which created the conditions needed for his influence in Europe. Though not himself postmodern in any sense, his non-metaphysical revelational approach to providing foundations for knowledge made him attractive to many. So also today, in a period in which the putative lack of foundations for knowledge makes us vulnerable to nihilism, reassurances based on optimistic assessments of human nature are not going to satisfy. What is needed is a theology that, without violating newly accepted canons of postmodern reflection, is able to address the situation created by those canons. Many are finding such a theology in Karl Barth.

Barth, Karl, *Church Dogmatics* (13 vols.; 1936–69)

—— *The Epistle to the Romans* (1933).

—— *The Göttingen Dogmatics: Instruction in the Christian Religion* (1991).

Busch, Eberhard, *Karl Barth: His Life from Letters and Autobiographical Texts* (1976).

Gay, Peter, *Weimar Culture* (1968).

Hunsinger, George, *How to Read Karl Barth* (1991).

McCormack, Bruce, *Karl Barth's Critically Realistic Dialectical Theology: Its Genesis and Development, 1909–1936* (1995).

—— 'Beyond Nonfoundational and Postmodern Readings of Barth: Critically Realistic Dialectical Theology', *Zeitschrift für dialektische Theologie*, 13 (1997).

—— 'Grace and Being: The Role of God's Gracious Election in Karl Barth's Theological Ontology', in John B. Webster (ed.), *Cambridge Companion to Karl Barth* (2000).

Roberts, Richard, *A Theology on its Way? Essays on Karl Barth* (1991).

Steiner, George, *Martin Heidegger*, 2nd edn. (1978).

Webster, John, *Barth's Ethics of Reconciliation* (1995).

XXI

Reinhold and H. Richard Niebuhr (1892–1971 and 1894–1962)

ROGER L. SHINN

The Niebuhr brothers, along with the German-American Paul Tillich, are often regarded as the most influential American theologians of the mid-20th century. In the turbulent theological climate of North American Christianity, such a judgement is bound to be controversial. Both Niebuhrs broke out of the categories of the fundamentalist-modernist controversy that shook the American churches in the early part of the century. The combatants in that continuing struggle looked to other intellectual leaders, but often took account of the Niebuhrs as makers and shakers of Christian thought. Ironically, the two were not in the strictest sense theologians. Both did their primary work in Christian ethics; neither wrote a treatise on the major Christian doctrines. But in a cataclysmic era of world history their response to events and to culture had a considerable impact upon church and society, including more systematic theologians.

The brothers grew up in a parsonage of the Evangelical Synod of North America, a church that inherited both the Lutheran and Calvinist traditions of Germany. Both went to a college and theological seminary of that church, then continued studies at the more ecumenical

Yale University Divinity School. Both were men in motion, responding in different ways to a changing history. Hence it is appropriate to treat them individually, with attention to their biographical developments, before making some comparisons.

Reinhold Niebuhr 🌿

Reinhold Niebuhr began his professional career with a thirteen-year pastorate in Detroit, Michigan (1915–28). There, in the motor capital of the world, he met the problems and conflicts of urban-industrial society. He championed the cause of labour in the automobile industry and chaired the mayor's Race Committee. His book, *Reflections from the Notebook of a Tamed Cynic* (1929), records pastoral experiences from 1915 to 1928 and gives hints of ideas he would later make famous. In 1928 he joined the faculty of Union Theological Seminary in New York and, a little later, the Graduate Faculty of Columbia University. Soon America faced the Great Depression, and Niebuhr entered the ten years that shook his world, as he called them in 1939. At Union he met the British fellow, Ursula Keppel-Compton, whom he married in 1931. The two became devoted marital partners and intellectual companions.

In 1932 Niebuhr published his epochal book, *Moral Man and Immoral Society*. It was a polemic against the 'liberalism' that he had earlier advocated. He argued that people who may be genial and generous in personal relations are often stubborn partisans of their own class or race or nation. He maintained that liberal optimism fails when reason and religion, hailed as the hopes for a better world, become the instruments of power, intensifying rather than moderating factional strife. There was more than a tinge of Marxism in the book, although Niebuhr kept a critical distance from Marx.

Soon he was urging a more radical politics and more conservative religious convictions than prevailed in American society. That meant a shattering of stereotypes, in which both politics and religion clustered in liberal-radical or conservative groupings. The effect was to disturb conventional thinking and to create new alliances and new debates. Niebuhr ran for Congress as a socialist in 1932, after assuring his seminary president that he would not give up teaching because he had no chance of winning. He founded the Fellowship of Socialist Christians and edited its quarterly, *Radical Religion*, later *Christianity and Society*.

Theologically, he won an international reputation with his address at the Oxford Conference on Life and Work (1937) and enhanced it with his Gifford Lectures at Edinburgh (1939), published as *The Nature and Destiny of Man*. Niebuhr's mature thought drew on many sources, especially three improbable partners in dialogue: Augustine, Marx, and Kierkegaard. In Augustine he appreciated the interest in the long drama of history with its ceaseless conflicts between good and evil, never to be resolved this side of the ultimate coming of God's kingdom. In Marx he found the importance of the grubby stuff of economic and political history, too often neglected by Christian thought. In Kierkegaard he found illumination of the anxieties of the self in its frailties, sin, and struggles for faith.

The rise of Nazism led to new moves in Niebuhr's political and theological life. As early as 1933 he resigned from the pacifist Fellowship of Reconciliation, of which he had been national chairman. In 1940 he left the Socialist Party, which stood aloof from the war. The next year he founded the bi-weekly *Christianity and Crisis*, to oppose the mingled quasi-pacifism and isolationism of much American Christianity and to relate theology to the contemporary world-historical struggles.

The following years brought a stream of writings on theology, politics, American history and culture, and international affairs. These were slowed but not stopped by serious illnesses, beginning with a stroke in 1952. Niebuhr modified his earlier moves towards more radical politics and more conservative theology, in both cases coming to appreciate some elements in the liberalism that he had once attacked.

Politically the evils of Nazism convinced him that the liberal values of freedom and tolerance, which he had always endorsed, deserved a stronger defence than he had earlier realized. Simultaneously, the social changes brought about by the New Deal in the United States, the Labour Party in Great Britain, and the social democratic parties of continental Europe showed him that liberal democracy had greater capacities for self-correction than he had once supposed. But he sustained his attacks on the liberal faith in progress and the neglect of attention to sin. Some advocates of neo-conservatism in the United States came to claim the heritage of Niebuhr, although on the American spectrum he remained left of centre and a biting critic of political reactionaries.

Theologically, also, he reclaimed elements of the liberal heritage that he had always taken for granted. Following the First Assembly of the World Council of Churches (Amsterdam, 1948), at which he and Karl Barth were major speakers, he entered into controversy with Barth, accenting the liberal elements in his own political and theological beliefs. During the Cold War his fierce opposition to Stalinist communism (involving further controversy with Barth) led to greater appreciation of American democracy, even though he continued to criticize its self-righteousness and urged patience in the prolonged co-existence necessary to avoid a nuclear war.

Niebuhr's thinking, never static, responded continuously to historical change. He characteristically advanced by correcting his own earlier thoughts. But four insights remained persistent throughout his mature career. First, he regarded theological language as symbolic, often mythological, to be understood 'seriously but not literally'. This brought attacks from conservatives who took literally biblical and traditional beliefs (e.g. original sin) and from liberals who dispensed with such beliefs, regarding Niebuhr as 'neo-orthodox', although he himself disliked that term.

Second, his beliefs about human nature included affirmations of the image of God in human personality, of the power and persistence of sin, and of human dependence on divine grace, both the common grace that sustains all human life and the special grace described by the bible and Christian tradition.

Third, he was indefatigably activist, an heir of the social gospel, but anti-utopian. The persistent fact of sin betrays all utopias, which breed fanaticism ('hard' utopias) or ineffective idealism ('soft' utopias). But, against despair, he refused to set limits on the possibilities of improving public life.

Fourth, the love–justice dialectic pervaded all his thought. Love without justice degenerates into sentimentality. But when love seeks justice, it moves into the conflicts of power that characterize human social life. Love, which is gracious and voluntary, exercises coercion in the enforcement of law and, most poignantly, in armed defence against aggression or revolution against tyranny. Thus love and justice exist in uneasy tension, yet each is incomplete without the other. Friends of US President Jimmy Carter (1976–80) say that he often quoted Niebuhr's statement that 'the sad job of politics is to bring justice to a sinful world'.

At the time of Niebuhr's death in 1971 the political scientist Hans Morgenthau had acclaimed him as America's 'greatest living political philosopher'. The Federal Bureau of Investigation maintained a file of 635 pages on him, telling more about its follies than about him, yet he was awarded the President's Medal for Freedom in 1964. He was widely known in Europe, and public figures in India and Indonesia acknowledged his influence. A published bibliography of his works ran to more than a thousand items, ranging from articles (some scholarly, some journalistic) to major books. His 'Christian realism', although rejected both by ethical perfectionists and by Christians who abjured political involvement, was the reference point for most Christian debates about social ethics. Although clearly Protestant, he sustained cordial relations with many Roman Catholics and Jews, sometimes joking about his frequent political efforts to get Jews and Catholics to outvote Protestants. Intellectuals quipped about 'atheists for Niebuhr'.

H. Richard Niebuhr 🌿

H. Richard Niebuhr, after earning his Ph.D. at Yale—a rite of passage that Reinhold ignored—became for three years president of Elmhurst College, then for four years a professor at Eden Theological Seminary, his alma maters. In 1931 he joined the faculty at Yale Divinity School, where he taught until his death in 1962.

In 1929 he jolted the American church with his first book, *The Social Sources of Denominationalism*. It was primarily a sociological study in the tradition of Ernst Troeltsch, who had been the subject of Niebuhr's doctoral dissertation. It showed that denominational divisions, often attributed to theology, are actually rooted in social realities—in class and caste, nation, region, and race. But if Niebuhr diminished the historical influence of doctrine, he displayed theological fervour in his attack on the 'hypocrisy' of denominationalism. Those who think of Reinhold as the polemicist and Richard as the quiet sage are still surprised at the sting in his attack on the moral failure of Christianity in its denominational divisiveness.

Eight years later in *The Kingdom of God in America* he pointed to a more creative role of the American churches. It was their faith in the Kingdom of God. He showed major variations in this faith: from the Puritan sovereignty of God to the evangelical reign of Christ in the human soul to the Social Gospel's kingdom on earth; but Niebuhr found in all of these a prophetic motif. This book includes the most-quoted sentence in all his writings, characterizing one form of liberal theology: 'A God without wrath brought men without sin into a kingdom without judgment through the ministrations of a Christ without a cross' (p. 193).

His next major work was more clearly theological. *The Meaning of Revelation* (1941) acknowledged the influence of both Troeltsch and Karl Barth. Troeltsch, the pluralist, relativized theological declarations, showing their roots in cultural particularities. Barth declared the radical authority of the Word of God, addressing and judging human creatures from above. Niebuhr drew together these contrasting themes. Revelation, he said, is the inward appropriation of a particular history, which becomes the centre of a continuing revolution in the religious community. Like Troeltsch he found no superhistorical vantage point from which to judge religions and assert the superiority of one's own. But in Barthian style he said that revelation is self-evidencing, not vindicated by any authority, empirical or rational, outside itself. Thus he affirmed, more modestly than most of the Christian tradition, that Christian insights are limited; yet he reached for universality in holding that God, known by Christians in their limited history, is the God of all histories.

In *Christ and Culture* (1951), Niebuhr again drew together his sociological and theological interests. Christians, he said, are constantly trying to relate Christ to the culture in which they live. Over the expanse of history he found five principal ways of relating the two. Between two limiting positions, 'Christ against culture' and 'Christ of culture' he discerned three mediating possibilities. Of these, 'Christ the transformer of culture' was his favourite. Yet he found all five to be important partners in a dialogue that is 'unconcluded and inconclusive'. The continuing quest was important to the man who had earlier described revelation as 'continuous revolution'.

All these works reveal a concern for the church, not always evident in academic theologians. Niebuhr made it quite explicit when he took leave from academia in order to direct a study of theological education in the United States and Canada, sponsored by the American Association of Theological Schools. Once again he brought together his interests in sociology and theology. The study, involving many people and institutions, produced three books, *The Purpose of the Church and Its Ministry* (1956), and two others assembled by the team that he headed.

The final book published during his lifetime was *Radical Monotheism and Western Culture* (1960). Here he modified the radical historical accent of earlier works and, in a turn to metaphysics, described God as 'the principle of being itself' (p. 32). Some scholars saw here the influence of Paul Tillich, whose early book, *The Religious Situation*, Niebuhr had translated from German in 1932. Others saw the influence of his old love, the American Puritan Jonathan Edwards.

While friends and admirers were still grieving over Niebuhr's death, *The Responsible Self* appeared in 1963. Many were surprised to find it a book of 'moral philosophy', in conscious resistance to the neo-orthodoxies that isolated theology from philosophy. He understood moral decisions as the acts of persons responding to other persons and to God in an ever-changing history. He sought to chart a path that avoids both traditional ethical absolutism (which generally absolutizes the particularities of a partisan group) and the glibness of situation ethics.

Continuing influence 🌿

Both Niebuhrs fell into some neglect in the 1960s, with the rise of theologies of liberation and diverse ethical movements. Their self-critical pilgrimages and anti-utopianism seemed tame to more messianic enthusiasts. But with the fading of many partisan hopes came a renewed influence of the brothers. A flurry of posthumous books, by them and about them, thrust both back into the midst of discussion. Republication of their older books kept their ideas in circulation long after the shorter influence of most, though not all, of the thinkers who for a time displaced them.

The brothers had different and complementary styles. Reinhold in his exuberance would seize on an idea, put it forth, then revise or criticize it in later publications. Richard tested his ideas in teaching and reformulated them many times before putting them in print. The two esteemed and admired each other. Occasional dabblers in psychobiography have sought signs of sibling rivalry. Given their searching doctrines of sin, the Niebuhrs probably believed that no brothers since Cain and Abel have been utterly free of such rivalry. But each dedicated a book to the other. Each occasionally teased the other as each poked fun at himself, and the affection of the teasing was evident to all who observed the smiles and the tone of voice.

On rare occasions they entered into public or semi-public controversy. An example in 1941 was a meeting of the Fellowship of Socialist Christians. Hitler's blitzkrieg had hit Norway, Denmark, and Belgium, made France a puppet state, and bombed British cities. Reinhold publicly advocated American support of Britain at the risk of involvement in war. Richard said that 'the real issue' for the church was not whether to go to war. It was 'to help the nation to become morally fit either to stay out or to enter into war'. Years later Richard diagnosed the difference: Reinhold was called to the reform of culture while Richard was called to the reformation of the church. A consequence was that Reinhold was the conspicuous public figure, whose opinions were heard (though often rejected) by high government officials. But he sometimes acclaimed Richard as a superior scholar. A later generation would dishonour the Niebuhrs if it fixed their ideas as final truth. Both brothers would rather be known as pilgrims.

Niebuhr, H. Richard, *Faith on Earth*, ed. Richard R. Niebuhr (1989).
—— *Theology, History, and Culture: Major Unpublished Writings*, ed. William Stacy Johnson (1996).
Niebuhr, Reinhold, *The Nature and Destiny of Man*, i. *Human Nature* (1941); ii. *Human Destiny* (1943).
—— *The Children of Light and the Children of Darkness: A Vindication of Democracy and a Critique of its Traditional Defense* (1944).
—— *The Irony of American History* (1952).
—— *The Self and the Dramas of History* (1955).

Brown, Charles C., *Niebuhr and his Age: Reinhold Niebuhr's Prophetic Role in the Twentieth Century* (1992).

Niebuhr, Ursula M. (ed.), *Remembering Reinhold Niebuhr: Letters of Reinhold and Ursula M. Niebuhr* (1991).

Robertson, D. B., *Reinhold Niebuhr's Works: A Bibliography*, rev. edn. (1983).

Stone, Ronald H., *Professor Reinhold Niebuhr: A Mentor to the Twentieth Century* (1992).

Thieman, Ronald F. (ed.), *The Legacy of H. Richard Niebuhr* (1991).

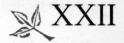

XXII

Karl Rahner (1904–1984)

KAREN KILBY

Rahner was one of the most important Roman Catholic theologians of the 20th century and a major influence on Vatican II.

Born in Freiburg im Breisgau, west Germany, Karl Rahner entered the Society of Jesus in 1922, three weeks after finishing secondary school. He followed the usual pattern of Jesuit training, and in 1932 was ordained a priest. From 1934 to 1936 he did doctoral work in philosophy at Freiburg, where he also attended the seminars and lectures of the existentialist philosopher Martin Heidegger. In 1936 he completed a doctorate in theology at Innsbruck in Austria, and subsequently taught at Innsbruck, Munich, and Münster. During the 1950s and early 1960s the orthodoxy of Rahner's work came under suspicion from Rome, but he was appointed as a theological expert at Vatican II by the German bishops, and his role, particularly through the advice he gave them, significantly affected its outcome. Though he retired from teaching in 1971 he continued to publish until his death in 1984.

At the time of Rahner's training the Catholic intellectual world was dominated by neo-scholasticism, a system of philosophy and theology based on the thought of Thomas Aquinas, and in particular Aquinas as seen through the lens of 16th- and 17th-century commentators. Neo-scholasticism offered something very like a closed intellectual system in which everything, or at least everything of any importance, was already worked out. It was the intellectual face of a Catholicism that had turned in upon itself and adopted a largely negative and defensive attitude towards the developments of the modern world, towards non-Catholic churches, and towards religions other than Christianity. Much of Rahner's work can be understood as an effort to fight the narrowness of this prevailing neo-scholasticism, opening it up from within, showing that the system contained more unresolved issues and open questions than was commonly supposed, and that it in fact left room for positive engagements with contemporary thought and with the modern world.

A variety of influences contributed to the shape of Rahner's theology. One of these was neo-scholasticism itself, which provided the framework within which much of Rahner's thinking took place as well as the framework against which he struggled. Rahner's time studying under Heidegger was also significant, though its influence is arguably more noticeable on the vocabulary than on the content of his thought. Probably the most important philosophical influence on his work came through his study of the writings of Joseph Maréchal, a Belgian Jesuit philosopher of the previous generation. Maréchal interpreted Aquinas in the light of Kant (which gave rise to the name 'Transcendental Thomists' for his followers) and thereby opened up the possibility of making a positive use of modern philosophy without abandoning the Catholic allegiance to Aquinas. Rahner's theology was also shaped by his immersion in patristic and medieval spirituality, and above all by the Spiritual Exercises and other writings of Ignatius Loyola, the 16th-century saint and founder of the Jesuits.

Early in his career Rahner produced two significant philosophical works, *Spirit in the World*, which began life as his failed Ph.D. thesis in philosophy, and *Hearer of the Word*, originally a set of lectures in the philosophy of religion. The most important idea to come out of these early volumes is that of the *Vorgriff auf esse*, usually translated the 'pre-apprehension of being'. Undergirding and accompanying every human act of knowing and willing, Rahner argued, there is a certain awareness of the infinity of being, and therefore of God. God can never be known directly; he can never be an object for the mind in the way that a chair or a table can be; but when we know some particular thing, or will some finite value, we are never *merely* knowing or choosing the particular, finite being, but always at the same time reaching beyond it, towards the whole of being, and therefore towards God. Without this 'reaching beyond', knowledge or choice of individual objects could not occur in the first place: the *Vorgriff auf esse* is a condition of the possibility of all our knowing and willing. Rahner's rather daring claim, then, is that everyone is in some sense aware of God whether they realize it or not, and that all our most pedestrian dealings with the world would in fact be impossible without this awareness.

Apart from these two early philosophical volumes and *Foundations of Christian Faith*, a major systematic work published after his retirement, Rahner's energies were spent on shorter pieces, and it is in his essays and brief monographs that his most characteristic and important work is to be found. Many of the essays are collected in the twenty-three volumes of the *Theological Investigations*.

Rahner dealt with an immense range of themes, and his theology defies summary. The topics on which he published include the Trinity, the Incarnation, the church, the sacraments, Mary, angels, indulgences, heresy, the development of doctrine, concupiscence, poetry, childhood, power, leisure, sleep, pluralism, mystery, symbol, death, devotion to the sacred heart of Jesus, devotion to the saints, asceticism, prayer, Ignatian mysticism, the relationship of Christianity to Marxism, to evolutionary theory, and to psychotherapy (psychology), the relationship between nature and grace, between scripture and tradition, between exegesis and theology, and between the papacy and the episcopate. The list could easily be continued. On the whole this work did not emerge as part of any overarching plan; many of the essays were occasioned by contemporary theological debates or contemporary pastoral problems, by pronouncements of church authorities, by invitations to give lectures, lead retreats or participate in conferences, or simply by Rahner's teaching duties.

In spite of the tremendous range and variety of Rahner's thought, there are certain interlocking themes to which he frequently returns and which play a pivotal role in many, though not all, of his pieces. Key to what could be called the core of his thought are his conception of God's self-communication, his theory of the supernatural existential, and his preoccupation with the relationship between 'transcendental' and 'categorical' experience.

Rahner refers quite frequently to the notion of divine self-communication. God chooses to give himself, to communicate himself, to the world: he does not give some particular thing, or communicate some information *about* himself, but actually gives his very self. This serves as an overarching concept by means of which Rahner can both interpret and unite a variety of traditional topics of theological reflection. Grace, for instance, is to be understood not, or not primarily, as some particular help or some created gift, but as God's giving of himself to the depths of the individual, and revelation has to do most fundamentally with God's communication *of* himself rather than a communication of any propositions *about* himself. In the Incarnation the divine self-communication reaches a point of absolute definitiveness in history. In the beatific vision it reaches its absolute fulfilment. And this self-communication is the purpose of creation: God creates the world precisely so as to give himself to it; he brings that which is other than himself into being in order to unite it with himself.

The 'supernatural existential' is a related notion: Rahner uses it to specify what this divine self-communication means in the life of the individual. The term itself reflects the unusual interplay of neo-scholasticism and Continental philosophy characteristic of much of Rahner's writing: the notion of an 'existential', a fundamental element in human existence which is a constant feature of experience rather than one among its objects, Rahner derives from Heidegger; 'supernatural', on the other hand, is used as a technical term of scholasticism—the supernatural existential was first introduced, in fact, in Rahner's contribution to a debate among Roman Catholic theologians over the relationship between nature and grace. At issue in this debate was whether human beings have 'by nature' a desire for that which is beyond the capacity of their nature—whether human nature includes an unconditional desire for the beatific vision, for a kind of relationship with God that can only be attained if we are lifted beyond ourselves by grace. Proponents of what was called the *nouvelle théologie*, in particular Henri de Lubac, defended the existence of such a desire, and accused the traditional neo-scholastics who denied it of making grace irrelevant and superfluous; neo-scholastics countered that the *nouvelle théologie* undermined the gratuity of grace, turning it into something *owed* to human beings. Rahner sought to develop a third option acceptable to both sides of the debate. His proposed solution hinged on a distinction between 'pure nature', in the theological sense as that which is distinguished from grace and the supernatural, and 'concrete nature', our human nature as we actually know it. As we concretely experience our nature, Rahner suggested, we do indeed find at its very heart, as the 'central and abiding existential of man', an unconditional desire for grace and for the beatific vision. But this is only because our nature is *already* shaped by its situation in a world created for the sake of God's gracious self-communication. This central existential, then, which is everywhere found as part of our concretely experienced nature, is in fact already *super*natural.

In later writings Rahner presents the supernatural existential not just as an inbuilt *desire* for grace and the beatific vision but as a universal *experience* of grace, or at least of the offer of grace. He maintains that all human beings are not only constantly aware of God by means of the *Vorgriff*, but also that they are constantly experiencing God as graciously offering himself. One does not have to recognize this experience explicitly *as* an experience of grace in order to accept (or reject) it: we accept or reject the offer, according to Rahner, in so far as on some level we fundamentally accept or reject ourselves.

A recurring issue in Rahner's theology is how this grace universally experienced in the depths of consciousness is related to the concrete claims, institutions, and practices of Christianity, to the bible, the church, and the sacraments, to historical revelation, and to Christ himself. Rahner's reflections in this connection are rich, varied, and developed in a variety of contexts, but in the broadest of terms they revolve around his understanding of the relationship between what he calls transcendental and categorial experience. These terms do not refer to two distinct sets of experiences, but to two levels he takes to be present in all experience. In all our dealings with concrete objects and people, with all that is finite and describable in categories (our categorial experience) we are always at the same time going beyond—'transcending' the finite and the nameable. Our awareness of God, our experience of grace, our sense of responsibility and our freedom, our fundamental choice of who to be, these all belong to the realm of our 'transcendental experience', impossible to pin down precisely and isolate as particular experiences among others and yet ever-present in our most mundane affairs. It is in the nature of transcendental experience, Rahner insists, that it must always somehow find expression and concrete realization on the categorial level, even though the transcendental can never be entirely caught and pinned down in words, categories, or finite realities. And this is true of God's self-communication as well: it is given in our transcendental experience as the supernatural existential, but it must also have a categorial expression. It must be realized and made concrete in history, in particular events, texts, societies, and institutions. Because God's self-communication is everywhere present and active, it finds categorial expression to some degree in all societies and cultures. The definitive and divinely guaranteed expression, however, occurs in Christ, and so also in the society and institution that derive from him, that is in the church.

The theory of the anonymous Christian, for which Rahner is most widely known and most frequently criticized, is closely connected to this core of ideas. Rahner's proposal that atheists and practitioners of other religions may in fact be Christians 'anonymously' is not a free-standing attempt to grapple with the problems of religious diversity and interreligious dialogue, but a proposition that flows directly from some of the central elements of his thought. If grace is universally offered in the depths of consciousness, if it is possible to accept this grace without explicitly realizing that this is what one is doing, and if, as Rahner also maintains, all grace is the grace of Christ, then it becomes possible to suggest that those of any religious persuasion whatsoever may without realizing it be saved through their acceptance of the grace of Christ. There is, it should be noted, no reason to suppose that they will them-selves concur in this reading of their situation, given that they do not begin from the same premises as does Rahner, but persuading others to regard themselves as Christians is not the purpose of Rahner's theory.

Like any important and complex thinker, Rahner has come to rep-resent different things to different people. To those interested in prob-lems of religious diversity he is known primarily for the theory of the anonymous Christian, and is presented as the classic exponent of 'inclusivism'. To others he is above all a 'transcendental' theologian, who not only gives a central place to the notion of transcendental ex-perience, but also maintains that theology must follow philosophy in ad-opting a transcendental method, something which critics see as tending to undermine the historical concreteness and particularity of Christian-ity. To yet others Rahner represents a particular point on the spec-trum of Roman Catholic theology: conservative and tradition-bound in comparison to Hans Küng, dangerously modern and of questionable orthodoxy from the point of view of Joseph Ratzinger and Hans Urs von Balthasar.

Rahner, K., *Hearer of the Word* (1941), ET (1994).

—— *Spirit in the World* (1957), ET (1968).

—— *Theological Investigations* ET (1963–92), i–xxiii.

—— *Foundations of Christian Faith* (1976), ET (1989).

Dych, W. V., *Karl Rahner* (1992).

Kilby, K., *Karl Rahner* (1997).

O'Donovan, L. (ed.), *A World of Grace: An Introduction to the Themes and Foundations of Karl Rahner's Theology* (1980).

Vorgrimler, H., *Karl Rahner: His Life, Thought and Works* (1966).

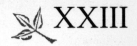

XXIII

Hans Urs von Balthasar

(1905–1988)

Edward T. Oakes

One of the most prolific, creative, and wide-ranging theologians of the 20th century, the Swiss Catholic Hans Urs von Balthasar spent his entire life outside the guild of academic theology. His doctorate was in German literature, not theology, and he never held an academic post or attended theological congresses and the like. This may partly explain why his large volume of writing, expressing a daring originality of vision, has had as yet relatively little impact. Moreover, this very originality makes his work hard to categorize and is thus apt to inhibit any immediate reception and appropriation.

His theological isolation also has certain biographical roots: born into an upper-middle class family of noble stock (hence the *von* in his name), he quickly became known for precocious talents in literature and music and received a doctorate in *Germanistik* from the University of Zürich in 1929. At the time he seemed destined for a career in bourgeois academia until he made a retreat in the Black Forest where he heard a call to become a Catholic priest in the Society of Jesus (Jesuits). During his pre-ordination philosophical and theological training in the 1930s he acquired an intense aversion for the 'sawdust Thomism' of the anti-modernist neo-scholastic manuals that were then standard in seminary teaching. After his ordination in Munich in 1936, he was assigned there to the editorial staff of *Stimmen der Zeit*, the Jesuit monthly; but approaching war and Nazi suspicions of his doctoral thesis *Die Apocalypse der deutschen Seele* (which uncannily anticipated the coming catastrophe) forced his return to Switzerland, where he became chaplain to the students of the University of Basel. There he met the twice-married Protestant physician Adrienne von Speyr, who converted to Roman Catholicism under his tutelage. Much influenced by her visions and mystical experiences, which he recorded at length, he left the Society of Jesus to join her in founding a 'secular institute', a relatively new form of religious life under vows but without the traditional external props of distinctive dress or life in common.

One of the major works of this institute was the publishing firm of Johannes Verlag. Besides most of Balthasar's own works, it published Hans Küng's doctoral thesis, *Justification* (a reconciliation between Karl Barth and the Council of Trent), and Karl Rahner's challenging *Free Speech in the Church*. Balthasar's own study, *The Theology of Karl Barth*, and his *Razing the Ramparts*, an attack on the fortress mentality common in the Roman Catholic Church of that time, combined with these publications to place him among the 'progressive theologians' of the *nouvelle théologie*, under whom he had in fact studied at Lyons before his ordination.

But after Vatican II—in which, characteristically, he had not taken part—he grew suspicious of certain theological trends claiming support from the Council and founded the journal *Communio* explicitly to counteract the post-conciliar liberal journal *Concilium*. Later in *Cordula* (ET: *The Moment of Christian Witness*), he sharply attacked Rahner's theory of the 'anonymous Christian' and publicly defended the Holy See's withdrawal of Küng's authorization to teach Catholic theology; and towards the end of his life he became known as 'the

Pope's favourite theologian'. He died two days before he was to receive the Cardinal's red hat from John Paul II.

Whatever may have been the effect of these apparent shifts in relation to the climate of opinion, the relatively small response to Balthasar's theology has also been due to its peculiarly anti-systematic bent, a trait that gives his work a strange elusiveness, making it extremely hard to categorize. Perhaps most crucially, the work of assimilation has to clear an additional hurdle: his claim that modernity's dearest presuppositions must be turned inside out. For Balthasar, the often strained relations between secular culture and Christian thought stem fundamentally not from Christianity's failure to keep in step with history but from modernity's habit of seeing things from the wrong end of the telescope. Indeed Balthasar's critique of the Enlightenment bears interesting resemblances to that found in many postmodernist thinkers—not surprising, considering how greatly he was influenced by Nietzsche. But in contrast with the extreme perspectivism that has become the standard position of postmodernism, Balthasar will always insist that there is a whole that governs communication across the partial perspectives seen by the finite mind: perspectives are partial *because* there is a whole that exceeds our partial grasp. Indeed, this is the source of his polemic against all systematic thought: that it pretends to have captured the whole in a graspable 'system'.

Soon after leaving the Society of Jesus in 1950 Balthasar conceived the project of writing a theological trilogy that would transpose all of theology into aesthetic, dramatic, and veridical terms, corresponding to the traditional Platonic transcendental properties of Being: the Beautiful, the Good, and the True—*and in that order*. This trilogy was consciously conceived to counteract what Balthasar regarded as the deleterious influence of Kant's three Critiques, the *Critique of Pure Reason*, *Critique of Practical Reason*, and *Critique of Judgement*, which significantly went in the opposite direction. Balthasar conceived this project because, again like so many postmodernists, he regarded the obsession with epistemological issues that marked modernity, from the time of Descartes, as a fundamental mistake. Much closer in this regard to Aristotle, who saw epistemology as reflection on the implications of the knowledge we already know we possess, Balthasar insisted that there can be no reflection on the *truth* of Christian revelation (Part 3) until it is lived out in committed *action* (Part 2), which a Christian will never feel called to do without having first perceived revelation in all its inherent *beauty* (Part 1). For it is the fundamental property of the beautiful to elicit its own quasi-erotic response, a response that will inevitably call the person out of himself and into committed action; and that action will then afford the person a variety of perspectives to serve as the basis for a *later* reflection on the truth of the revelation that elicited the response.

Inside this overarching structure certain other themes emerge, many of which also show Balthasar's deep anti-Kantianism. For example, it is a fundamental thesis of Kant's that religion must be able to justify itself before the bar of 'reason alone'. But Balthasar's own aesthetic starting-point insists that the Particular (for example, an event of history) gives a deeper insight into reality than does the (abstract) Universal of reason. We see this especially in his christology, where, in a fascinating image, he insists that the claim of Jesus to be 'the way, the truth, and the life' (John 14: 6) is equivalent to the whitecap on a wave claiming to be the sea itself: one phenomenon inside the world of Becoming has claimed to be Being itself ('before Abraham was, I am').

To understand that claim (in Balthasar's terminology a claim to *'absolute* singularity', defined as one that is, on the face of it, absurd and thus a scandal for universalizing reason), one must first look at such 'relative singularities' as great works of art: 'Great works of art appear like inexplicable eruptions on the stage of history,' he once said in a lecture later published as *Two Say Why*. 'Sociologists are as unable to calculate the precise day of their origin as they are to explain in retrospect why they appeared when they did. . . . [Art's] unique utterance becomes a universal language; and the greater a work of art, the more extensive the cultural sphere it dominates will be' (pp. 20–1).

The image of wave and sea also proves helpful in trying to understand how Christ's death and Resurrection can reach, salvifically, to the ends of the world. How can the impact of one historical figure, Jesus of Nazareth, reach out to all the rest of history, both the history that precedes and that follows his life? Altering the metaphor slightly, Balthasar answers that question by comparing the impact of any one human being in history to the ripple effect of a stone dropped into the sea. But with all other human beings the ripple effect eventually fades and dies out; so there must be something about the 'stone' of Jesus that differs in its radiating power.

Hegel once quoted a Swabian proverb to the effect that 'something has been true for so long it stopped being true'. This is why he insisted that theology, because it is so reliant on an ever-receding historical revelation, must let itself be transposed into the a-historical and universal categories of philosophy. But Balthasar answers Hegel by asserting that the ripple effect of Jesus' stone continues to radiate outwards because, when it plunged all the way to the bottom of the sea on Holy Saturday (that is, when Christ descended into hell), it landed, so to speak, with a thud that continues to reverberate. And that can only happen if the 'weight' of that single, particular stone serves as the counterweight (*Schwergewicht*) outweighing all the other truths and sufferings of the world, which is impossible unless this 'plunge' takes place within the very life of the Trinity. Only then does the centre where the stone was dropped continue to reverberate and radiate outwards. Moreover, that outward radiation moves concentrically in such a way as to influence *previous* history as well. This for Balthasar is the real meaning of the scriptural doctrine of Christ's descent into hell, where according to the Petrine tradition he rescues the 'spirits in prison who disobeyed God *long ago*' (1 Pet. 3: 19–20; see also 1 Pet. 4: 5–6).

These fascinating images of stone, wave, and sea clearly lead to a quasi-Origenistic vision of the possible redemption of *all* these 'disobedient spirits in prison'. This is because in his descent into hell Jesus experiences *all* that is hellish about the world in its otherness and divergence from God—whether that difference was willed through sin or results from creation's finite, non-divine status. Christ's descent means that ultimately hell is, in Balthasar's famous dictum, 'a christological place,' where finite sinners can, in their finitude, experience in a partial way what Christ himself experienced totally. And since any experience of Christ is by definition salvific, we may at least hope for the salvation of all.

These ideas are indeed daring and highly speculative and have led Rahner, among others, to accuse Balthasar of indulging in a 'Schellingesque projection into God of division, conflict, godlessness, and death'. According to Rahner, God must, if the word 'God' is to continue to have any meaning at all, enter history in a way that does not lock God into its horror; whereas for Balthasar God transforms that horror by incorporating suffering and rejection into the trinitarian process itself. And for Balthasar that process was fully realized when God raised Jesus from the dead—that is, when God rescued him from the hell to which he had been condemned *by God*. For 'it was impossible that Hades keep its hold on him' (Acts 2: 24, Western text).

> **von Balthasar**, **Hans Urs**, *Herrlichkeit*; ET, *The Glory of the Lord* (7 vols.; 1982–91).
> —— *Theodramatik*; ET, *Theo-Drama* (5 vols.; 1988).
> —— *Theologik*; ET, *Theo-Logic* (3 vols.; 2001).
> **Capol**, C., *Hans Urs von Balthasar: Bibliographie, 1925–1990* (1990).
> **Chapp**, **Larry S.**, *The God Who Speaks: Hans Urs von Balthasar's Theology of Revelation* (1996).
> **Oakes**, E. T., *Pattern of Redemption: The Theology of Hans Urs von Balthasar*, 2nd edn. (1997).

O'Hanlon, G., *The Immutability of God in the Theology of Hans Urs von Balthasar* (1990).

Riches, J. (ed.), *The Analogy of Beauty: The Theology of Hans Urs von Balthasar* (1986).

REFERENCE BOOKS FROM OXFORD

Partner volume to *Key Thinkers in Christianity*:

CHRISTIAN THOUGHT: A BRIEF HISTORY
Edited by Adrian Hastings, Alistair Mason, and Hugh Pyper

What does it mean to be a Christian at the dawn of the third millennium? What did it mean to be a Christian at the dawn of the first millennium? In 13 chronologically arranged chapters, through East and West, *Christian Thought: A Brief History* charts the path Christian thinkers have taken over the last 2,000 years searching for answers to some of the basic questions concerning existence and creation that have been churning in the minds of great thinkers for years.

The 13 chapters that make up this Brief History are drawn from the highly acclaimed *Oxford Companion to Christian Thought*, and are written by distinguished theologians and Church historians from both sides of the Atlantic, themselves all notable thinkers. They take the reader on a journey from Pre-Constantinian times to the end of the 20th century. It's a journey not simply through time, however, but across different traditions of Christian thought—Syriac and Armenian, as well as Eastern Orthodox and Western understandings.

Other titles published by Oxford University Press:

*THE CONCISE OXFORD DICTIONARY OF THE
CHRISTIAN CHURCH*—revised edition
Edited by E. A. Livingstone

Based on the highly acclaimed third edition of the *Oxford Dictionary of the Christian Church*, this revised edition contains over 5,000 entries providing full coverage of theology, denominations, the Church calendar, and the Bible.

'opens up the whole of Christian history, now with a wider vision than ever'
Robert Runcie, former Archbishop of Canterbury

THE CONCISE OXFORD DICTIONARY OF WORLD RELIGIONS
Edited by John Bowker

Abridged from the acclaimed *Oxford Dictionary of World Religions*, this is the most comprehensive and up-to-date dictionary of religion available in paperback. Written by an expert team of contributors, the volume contains over 8,200 entries containing unrivalled coverage of the major world religions, past and present.

'covers a vast range of topics and . . . is both comprehensive and reliable'
The Times

THEOLOGY: A VERY SHORT INTRODUCTION
David Ford

This Very Short Introduction provides both believers and non-believers with a balanced survey of the central questions of contemporary theology. David Ford's interrogative approach draws the reader into considering the principles underlying religious belief, including the centrality of salvation to most major religions, the concept of God in ancient, modern, and post-modern contexts, the challenge posed to theology by prayer and worship, and the issue of sin and evil. He also proves the nature of experience, knowledge, and wisdom in theology, and discusses what is involved in interpreting theological texts today.

'It is written in an extremely accessible, interesting and fresh style and this combined with its "safely" orthodox but balanced tone will make it a useful aid to assisting a range of people.'

Ray Gaston, *Theology*

AUGUSTINE: A VERY SHORT INTRODUCTION
Henry Chadwick

By his writings, the surviving bulk of which exceeds that of any other ancient author, Augustine came to influence not only his contemporaries but also the West since his time. This Very Short Introduction traces the development of Augustine's thought, discussing his reaction to the thinkers before him, and themes such as freedom, creation, and the Trinity.

'magisterial and highly readable'

Bookseller

HEGEL: A VERY SHORT INTRODUCTION—revised edition
Peter Singer

Many people regard Hegel's work as obscure and extremely difficult, yet his importance and influence are universally acknowledged. Peter Singer eliminates any excuse for remaining ignorant of the outlines of Hegel's philosophy by providing a broad discussion of his ideas, and an account of his major works.

Review from previous edition:
'an excellent introduction to Hegel's thought'

Sunday Times

KANT: A VERY SHORT INTRODUCTION—revised edition
Roger Scruton

Kant is arguably the most influential modern philosopher, but also one of the most difficult. Roger Scruton tackles his exceptionally complex subject with a strong hand, exploring the background to Kant's work, and showing why the *Critique of Pure of Reason* has proved so enduring.

Review from previous edition:
'Roger Scruton faced perhaps the most intractable task of all in giving an elementary account of Kant's philosophy . . . but he does it extremely elegantly and neatly.'

Listener

KIERKEGAARD: A VERY SHORT INTRODUCTION—
revised edition
Patrick Gardiner

Søren Kierkegaard, one of the most original thinkers of the 19th century, wrote widely on religious, psychological, and literary themes. This book shows how Kierkegaard developed his views in emphatic opposition to prevailing opinions. His arresting but paradoxical conception of religious belief is critically discussed, and Patrick Gardiner concludes this lucid introduction by showing how Kierkegaard has influenced contemporary thought.

THE BIBLE: A VERY SHORT INTRODUCTION
John Riches

This Very Short Introduction looks at the importance accorded to the Bible by different communities and cultures and attempts to explain why it has generated such a rich variety of uses and interpretations. It explores how the Bible was written, the development of the canon, the role of Biblical criticism, the appropriation of the Bible in high and popular culture, and its use for political ends.

PHILOSOPHY: A VERY SHORT INTRODUCTION
Edward Craig

How ought we to live? What really exists? How do we know? This book introduces important themes in ethics, knowledge, and the self, via readings from Plato, Hume, Descartes, Hegel, Darwin, and Buddhist writers. It emphasizes throughout the point of doing philosophy, explains how different areas of philosophy are related, and explores the contexts in which philosophy was and is done.

To find out more about these titles and many others, please visit our website www.oup.com or contact your local Oxford University Press office.